Success in Literacy Reading Tests

UNDERSTANDING
YEAR 8
COMPREHENSION

Excellent for all Students, Teachers, Coaches and Parents

Authors

Alan Horsfield *M.Ed., B.A., B.Ed., Dip.Sch.Admin., TESOL, Teaching Cert.*
Alan Horsfield has more than 35 years teaching experience in state and private schools in New South Wales and International Schools in Papua New Guinea. He was employed by UNSW (EAA) as an English Research Officer involved in the construction of school tests for English and Mathematics. Alan is a published writer of children's fiction, educational material and school texts.

Elaine Horsfield *M.A. (Theatre Studies), B.A. (Theatre Media), Teaching Cert.*
Elaine Horsfield has more than 25 years teaching experience in Primary Schools both with the New South Wales Department of Education and in International Schools in Papua New Guinea. She worked with secondary students as coordinator of the NSW Talent Development Project. Elaine is a published writer of children's poetry and educational books.

Editor:
Warwick Marlin B.Sc. Dip.Ed.

Publisher:
Five Senses Education
ABN: 16 001 414437
2/195 Prospect Highway
Seven Hills NSW Australia 2147
sevenhills@fivesenseseducation.com.au
www.fivesenseseducation.com.au

Trade Enquiries:
Phone (02) 9838 9265
Fax (02) 9838 8982
Email: fsonline@fivesenseseducation.com.au

Understanding Year 8 Comprehension
ISBN: 978-1-76032-165-9
1st Edition: August 2016
Copyright: Alan Horsfield © Five Senses Education Pty. Ltd. © Warwick Marlin

AUTHOR'S ACKNOWLEDGEMENTS

Warwick Marlin, my editor, whose advice and guidance have been very much appreciated.

Roger Furniss, at Five Senses Education for publishing my books.

And above all, to **Jones**, my typesetter, for a high standard of typesetting, layout and artwork. A very special thank you for your time, patience, attention to detail, and overall quality of your work.

PARENTS

This book tells you what the teacher often does not have the time to explain in detail - the intricacies of a wide variation in text types and the testing strategies used by Australian testing institutions to assess progress in Literacy. It will give you confidence to support your children by reinforcing what is being taught in schools and what is being tested, especially Reading Comprehension.

TEACHERS

This book introduces text types and test question types Australian students should understand to maximise internal and external Reading Tests. Reading tests may involve comprehension as well as related grammar questions. It eliminates the need to wade through lengthy curriculum documents and it provides a clear, easy to follow format for teachers to use. Teachers can confidently recommend this book to parents as it supports classroom activities and exercises.

B. Ed., Dip. Ed. PRIMARY SCHOOL TEACHERS

This book contains a variety of recognised school text types with question sets that will improve reading comprehension and improve results in reading tests. It acts as a quick reference book for teachers in the early years of teaching, when there is so much to learn.

Understanding Year 8 Comprehension
A. Horsfield © Five Senses Education © W. Marlin

AVAILABILITY OF MATHEMATICS BOOKS

All of the Mathematics books below have been produced by the same editor and publisher, and in many cases the same author (Warwick Marlin). Therefore they all incorporate the same high presentation and philosophy. They can be purchased directly from Five Senses Education, but they are also available in most educational bookshops throughout NSW and Australia (and also some selected bookshops in New Zealand).

New National Curriculum titles

The eight school titles listed directly below have been rewritten and updated in recent years to closely follow the New National Curriculum. **'All levels'** means that the books have been written for students of most ability groups (weak, average and gifted). The graded tests at the end of each chapter ensure that students of most ability groups are extended to their full potential.

❑	YEAR 1	ALL LEVELS
❑	YEAR 2	ALL LEVELS
❑	YEAR 3	ALL LEVELS
❑	YEAR 4	ALL LEVELS
❑	YEAR 5	ALL LEVELS
❑	YEAR 6	ALL LEVELS
❑	YEAR 7	ALL LEVELS
❑	YEAR 8	ALL LEVELS

Other titles in this series

The titles listed below are also available, but they will be fully updated during 2014 and 2015 to also closely follow the new curriculum. However, in the meantime, please note, that these books still adequately address the main features of the new syllabus. We firmly believe that the major topics explained in these titles, and our user friendly presentation and development of the different topics, will always continue to form the vital foundations for all future study and applications of mathematics. This is especially so for the titles up to, and including, year 10 advanced.

❑	YEAR 9 & 10	INTERMEDIATE
❑	YEAR 9 & 10	ADVANCED
❑	YEAR 11 & 12	GENERAL MATHS
❑	YEAR 11	EXTENSION 1
❑	YEAR 12	EXTENSION 1

Also by the same Author and Editor (Warwick Marlin)

❑	ESSENTIAL EXERCISES YEAR 1	ALL LEVELS
❑	ESSENTIAL EXERCISES YEAR 2	ALL LEVELS
❑	ESSENTIAL EXERCISES YEAR 3	ALL LEVELS
❑	ESSENTIAL EXERCISES YEAR 4	ALL LEVELS
❑	ESSENTIAL EXERCISES YEAR 5	ALL LEVELS
❑	ESSENTIAL EXERCISES YEAR 6	ALL LEVELS

Developed & written in 2012, this excellent new series of books closely follows the Australian National Curriculum.

CONTENTS

Page

INTRODUCTION

- Acknowledgments — iii
- Availability of books by the same editor & publisher — iv
- Understanding Year 8 English Testing — vi
- How to use this book effectively — vii
- Test sources — viii
- A brief summary of some question formats — ix
- A practice test — x

40 COMPREHENSION TESTS

These tests include narratives, poems, procedures, recounts, explanations, descriptions, reviews and reports. At the end of each test there is also a valuable and well explained literacy tip. — 1

ANSWERS – Reading Comprehension Tests — 83, 84

ANSWERS – Literacy Tip Exercises — 85, 86

"So it is with the children who learn to read fluently and well. They begin to take flight into whole new worlds as effortlessly as young birds take to the sky."

William James

Understanding Year 8 Comprehension
A. Horsfield © Five Senses Education © W. Marlin

UNDERSTANDING YEAR 8 ENGLISH TESTING

Advice for students

Now is the time to start thinking about a choice of subjects to study in the oncoming years. Some subjects are compulsory while others may not be offered or available at all schools. Check out your options. From Term 2 onwards, schools ask Year 8 students to select next year's electives. Choose subjects that you're good at and those that interest you. Discuss elective choices with your parents.

If you want to study specialised subjects later on, choose courses that lead to this goal.

If you have a particular career in mind, look at the qualifications that the industry or job requires and work back from there. If you are uncertain about what you want to do in the future and you want to keep your options open, select a good mix of subjects.

Make your own choices - **don't choose subjects because you want to be with friends.** Friendships change, schools change, families may move to new locations.

Advice for parents

Attend any parent-teacher meetings offered by the school. Meet your child's teachers. Find the best way to communicate with the school if there are issues. The year adviser may be a good first contact.

Remind your child that as soon as they find out they have an exam or assignment due, record the date appropriately and schedule study time in the period leading up to the event. This is an essential habit for students to develop.

Year 8 is a time when the student is becoming more independent and must accept greater responsibility for his/her progress. It is a time of shifting relationships for many teenagers. Balance is really important. Know who they're socialising with in person and online. Know when and how much time your child is spending looking at a screen. Find a balance between school and recreation as well as asleep, exercise and study time.

Even though 'homework' will take increasing amounts of the student's time, parents still need to provide positive support that stimulates interest and confidence in reading and writing. English is a compulsory subject. Throughout high school the student will continue to move from a more literal comprehension of text to an interpretive understanding of a wider variety of text types. What is implied becomes more and more important. Making rational judgments from various texts will be a developing skill. This transition will vary from student to student. At times, we all interpret text differently. It is also important to understand that we don't necessarily grasp the intended meaning on a first reading. Re-reading is an important strategy. This is important in test situations.

The NAPLAN testing program for Australian Schools treats three strands of English.

Reading tests, which include the comprehension of a variety
of text types,
Writing tests, which focus on writing a narrative, a persuasive
text or a recount,
Language Conventions tests, which include Spelling, Punctuation and Grammar.

> Year 8 is not a NAPLAN year. Year 9 is the last NAPLAN year.

This book focuses specifically on Reading but the skills learned in Reading can assist in the development of the student's Writing skills. The skills learned in the Language Convention strand can improve both Reading and Writing.

We have included a Literacy Tip (**Lit Tip**) component at the end of each set of questions. These may help with any Language Convention questions that come up in standardised reading tests as well adding 'tricks' that may improve the quality of Writing test responses.

Check out: http://www.australiancurriculum.edu.au/Year8

Sources: http://syllabus.bos.nsw.edu.au/stages/, Schoolatoz practical help for parents
Royal Borough of Greenwich; Advice for year 8 to 10 students

HOW TO USE THIS BOOK EFFECTIVELY

As stated, this book's primary aim is to improve Reading comprehension with some input into Language Conventions. Obviously the Speaking, Listening and Handwriting strands are not included.

The passages are not selected in any specific order but are intended to present a wide variation of text types. Those most likely to be part of the testing situation are treated more often. The text type is shown at the top of each passage as well as in the **List of comprehension passages and exercises** chart that follows on page 1.

There will be differences of focus from school to school, as teachers tend to select topics in varying sequences according to their program at a particular time in the year. Some students may also be involved in accelerated promotion, enrichment or remedial activities.

ABOUT THE EXERCISES

The intent of the 40 passages is to provide one passage per week for each school week. This should not impinge too much on the increasingly heavy obligations set by the school/class teacher for homework and research. There is one easier **practice passage** provided to make the child aware of a range of question types that may be encountered.

Children need not work through the exercisers from 1 to 40 in the order in which they are presented in this book. There is the option of practicing a particular text type, e.g. poetry.

The Comprehension Answers and the Lit Tip Answers are on separate pages at the back of the book.

Reading texts can be based on either **Factual** or **Literary** texts.

Year 8 question types often include the skills of:

- **Locating** such things as information, a sequence of events, literary techniques, grammar conventions and vocabulary features,

- **Identifying** genres, the purpose of a text, literary techniques, appropriate punctuation, word meanings,

- **Interpreting** visual information, multiple pieces of information, language style,

- **Inferring** next events in a text, reasons for a character's action, outcomes, the effect of tense and person, and

- **Synthesising** the tone of a text, the main idea in a text, a character's motivation, the writer's opinion, the intended audience for a text.

These above skills are more or less arranged in an order of difficulty.

Alan Horsfield M.Ed., B.A., B.Ed., Dip.Sch.Admin., TESOL, Teaching Cert.
Elaine Horsfield M. A. (Theatre Studies), B. A. (Theatre Media), Teaching Cert.

Understanding Year 8 Comprehension
A. Horsfield © Five Senses Education © W. Marlin

TEST SOURCES

The questions, information and practice provided by this book will benefit the student sitting for the following tests.

Externally produced tests

NAPLAN (National Assessment Program - Literacy and Numeracy) Used Australia wide.
PAT (-R) (Progressive Achievements Tests - Reading)
ICAS (International Competitions and Assessments for Schools) Run by EAA.
Selective schools and High Schools Placement Tests (Most states have tests specific to that state's educational policy.)
Scholarship Tests
ACER (Australian Council for Educational Research) Scholarship tests (Most states have tests specific to that state's educational policy)
AusVELS (Australian Curriculum in Victoria Essential Learning Standards)
Independent Assessment Agencies (e.g. Academic Assessment Services)
ISA (International Schools Assessment) run by ACER
There may be a number of other independent, external sources for literacy testing.

School (internally) produced tests
Information provided in this book may also be beneficial in certain competitions run by commercial enterprises.

The purpose of testing
Testing has a variety of purposes and the purpose will often determine the type of test administered. Tests may be used to
- determine what the student has learned
- rank students in order of ability
- select the most worthy student for a school or class
- determine the strength and weakness of classroom teaching
- determine any 'short-comings' in a school's educational program
- ascertain the effectiveness of certain teaching strategies
- evaluate the effectiveness of departmental/official syllabuses

The Australian Curriculum states that Year 8 students should be able to:
- Explore the ways that ideas and viewpoints in literary texts drawn from different historical, social and cultural contexts may reflect or challenge the values of individuals and groups(ACELT1626)
- Explore the interconnectedness of Country/Place, People, Identity and Culture in texts including those by Aboriginal and Torres Strait Islander authors(ACELT1806)
- Share, reflect on, clarify and evaluate opinions and arguments about aspects of literary texts (ACELT1627)
- Understand and explain how combinations of words and images in texts are used to represent particular groups in society, and how texts position readers in relation to those groups (ACELT1628)
- Recognise and explain differing viewpoints about the world, cultures, individual people and concerns represented in texts(ACELT1807)
- Recognise, explain and analyse the ways literary texts draw on readers' knowledge of other texts and enable new understanding and appreciation of aesthetic qualities(ACELT1629)
- Identify and evaluate devices that create tone, for example humor, wordplay, innuendo and parody in poetry, humorous prose, drama or visual texts (ACELT1630)
- Interpret and analyse language choices, including sentence patterns, dialogue, imagery and other language features in short stories, literary essays and plays(ACELT1767)

By the end of Year 8, students understand how the selection of text structures is influenced by the selection of language mode and how this varies for different purposes and audiences. Students explain how language features, images and vocabulary are used to represent different ideas and issues in texts.

Source: http://www.australiancurriculum.edu.au/Year8

A BRIEF SUMMARY OF SOME QUESTION FORMATS

Read the following as the text for a set of questions.

> When our neighbour, Mrs Faithful died unexpectedly last year after a short illness, the old Miss Longly sent a card in an envelope with a black border. My friend, Silvia Faithful showed it to me after her mother's funeral, which <u>seemed a simple affair - no bells and whistles</u>.
> Miss Clare Longly had written in the card. It was obviously written with a fountain pen. Her handwriting was full of loops and swirls and very neatly formed, but a bit old-fashioned looking. And so were the things she said in the card: May I offer the most sincere condolences on behalf of my sister and myself to Mr Faithful and his daughters, Clare and Heather on their grievous loss.
> It sounded rather starchy to me but at least she knew what to say. I would have simply blurted, in_____(4)_____ gush, 'Sorry,' if I happened to pass him in the street.
>
> **Adapted from an idea in** *Featherbys by Mary Steele 1993.*

Many tests are based on multiple-choice responses. You are most often given a choice of four possible answers (options) to choose from. Options may be in a vertical or horizontal format.

1. Who was it that died?
   A   Miss Longly
   B   Mr Faithful
   C   Silvia Faithful
   D   Mrs Faithful

> Some will take the form of a question. You may have to circle a letter or shade a box.

The question could have been framed so that you have to complete a sentence.
2. The person who died was

| Miss Longly | Mr Faithful | Silvia Faithful | Mrs Faithful |
| A | B | C | D |

Some questions may have to do with a word or phrase meanings.
3. What does the word *starchy* as used in the text imply?
   A   cheap   B   casual   C   formal   D   callous

4. Which words would best be suited for the space labelled (4)?
   A   a cordial   B   an unseemly   C   a bright   D   a tender

Some questions are called *free response* questions. You will have to write an answer.
5. Who was Clare's sister? _____(Write your answer on the line.)

Sometimes you might have to decide if something is TRUE or FALSE.
6. Tick the box if this statement is TRUE or FALSE according to information in the text.

   Miss Clare Longly was related to Mrs Faithful.   TRUE [   ]   FALSE [   ]

There will be times when you will have to read the whole text and make a judgement.
7. Which would be the most suitable title for the passage?
   A   The Funeral   B   Responses to Bereavement
   C   Mr Faithful's Loss   D   Street Encounter

8. There could be a question about the use of language in the text.
   The words, *bells and whistles* is an example of
   A   a metaphor   B   a simile   C   a colloquialism   D   an idiom

9. You might have to decide if, according to the text, a statement is FACT or OPINION.
   Are the words, *seemed a simple affair*, fact or opinion? _____(Write your answer here.)

You may have to make a judgement about a character or their motives.

10. Which word best describes how the narrator expected to react to any meeting with Mr Faithful?
    A   shaken   B   saddened   C   inappropriately   D   confidently

Answers: 1. D, 2. D, 3. C, 4. B, 5.Heather, 6. FALSE, 7. B, 8. D , 9.OPINION , 10. C

Understanding Year 8 Comprehension
A. Horsfield © Five Senses Education © W. Marlin

This is a practice page. (The answers follow the questions)

Read the extract *Spring Surprise.*

Spring Surprise

It was a glorious spring day. Looking at the sky was like being in a pale-blue balloon. The grass was so green it was almost as perfect as artificial turf. The air was cool with a promise of days on the beach to come.

Charlotte meandered up the gravel path, lost in the sights, smells and sounds of the moment. At the top of the path, where it turned right to go to the main gate and the concrete world, she stopped and turned to look back at the sky, the sea and the yacht club.

'The yacht club! I shouldn't be able to see the yacht club.'

It was only now she was outside the wood, as she called it, that she could see the missing trees. Or, rather, couldn't see the trees - because they were missing.

'What exactly is missing?' thought Charlotte as the familiar frown formed itself on her forehead.

She thought back to the last time she had been here.

'Three days ago, Wednesday; what exactly had been there that wasn't there now? Saplings! Or were they too big to be saplings? When do saplings stop being saplings and become trees?' Charlotte wrenched her thoughts back to the matter at hand.

The space that allowed her to see the yacht club had been filled by saplings (or small trees) with bright green leaves and small buds.

'I wonder what kind of trees they were?' she thought, before dragging her mind back to ____(6)____ matters.

Charlotte strode down to the treeless space and studied the ground. 'Grass.' The frown reappeared. 'No trees, just lots of grass.'

'Had there been trees here?' Charlotte questioned her memory, visualising what she was doing here last Wednesday.

She'd come down to watch some school friends practise their netball skills after school. About four-thirty, as a chill seeped into the air, she remembered that she had to buy some milk on her way home. The quickest way to the shop was the path through the park. Charlotte had briskly walked up the hill to get warm and remembered running her hand though the soft new leaves of - the missing saplings! They had been here!

Our thanks to John Andrews for permission to use this passage from the unpublished story Charlotte Holmes and the Knotty Problem.

Understanding narratives   Circle a letter or write an answer for questions 1 to 8.
(Note: The answers follow the questions for this Practice passage.)

1. What alerted Charlotte to the fact that a change had taken place in the park?
   - A   the grass had become much greener
   - B   she could see the yacht club and the sea
   - C   the gravel path turned right to go to the main gate
   - D   she saw that the saplings had become trees

2. What was Charlotte's initial reason for being in the park?
   - A   she wanted to watch classmates play netball
   - B   she intended to join in a game of netball
   - C   she was passing through the park to buy milk
   - D   she was investigating a strange event in the park

3. What is the simile in paragraph 1?
   Write your answer here? _____

4. How did Charlotte progress up the gravel path?
   - A   she walked slowly with heavy steps
   - B   she moved with determination
   - C   she ran at a moderate pace with short steps
   - D   she wandered at random

5. In which order did the events recoded in the passage take place?
   1. Charlotte has a clear view of the yacht club
   2. Charlotte buys milk from the shop
   3. Charlotte admires saplings planted in the park
   4. Charlotte watches some after-school activities

   A   **4, 1, 3, 2**   B   **3, 4, 1, 2**   C   **4, 3, 2, 1**   D   **1, 4, 3, 2**

6. A word has been deleted from the text.
   Which word would be best suited to the space (6)?
   - A   financial   B   lowly
   - C   practical   D   onerous

7. How did Charlotte most likely feel about her discovery?
   - A   cynical   B   baffled   C   defensive   D   animated

8. A suitable alternate title for the passage would be
   - A   Charlotte's confusion   B   The shady park
   - C   Errand to get milk   D   Pathway under the trees

Answers: 1. B   2. A   3. like being in a pale-blue balloon   4. D   5. C   6. C   7. B   8. A

Understanding Year 8 Comprehension
A. Horsfield © Five Senses Education © W. Marlin

Year 8 Comprehension Passages and Exercises

Each of the 40 passages has a set of eight questions - comprehension and language questions, based upon that text. Following the questions is a section called **Lit Tip** (short for Literacy Tips). These are gems of information that are intended to develop the child's responses to Language Conventions questions arising in texts and tests. They may also be beneficial when answering questions in Language Convention (Grammar) papers or when completing Writing assessment tasks.

Number	Text type	Title	Lit Tip	Page
1	Recount	Bennelong	Life dates	2 - 3
2	Procedure	Life jackets	Colloquialisms or idioms	4 - 5
3	Description	Coketown	Writing descriptions	6 - 7
4	Report	The Theia Hypothesis	*Majority* - correct usage	8 - 9
5	Poetry	Memory	The suffix *arian*	10 - 11
6	Recount	Gympie-Gympie stinging tree	The prefix *auto*	12 - 13
7	Book review	The Adventures of review	Using italics	14 - 15
8	Legends	The coconut tree legend	Use of *former* and *latter*	16 - 17
9	Explanation	Elimination Tournaments	Starting sentences with *And*	18 - 19
10	Applications	Applying for a Job	*Effect* or *affect*	20 - 21
11	Plans	Wind Spirit	Nautical terms	22 - 23
12	Itineraries	Savannahlander Itinerary	Plurals for years and initials	24 - 25
13	Narrative	The Hundred-Foot Journey	Mood (or atmosphere)	26 - 27
14	Explanation	What are water bears?	Morphemes	28 - 29
15	Report	The Vanilla Island	Initials, acronyms and brackets	30 - 31
16	Report	Space weather	Interjections	32 - 33
17	Explanation	Hammerheads	Nouns and gender	34 - 35
18	Poetry	Heat Wave	The prefix *para*	36 - 37
19	Exposition	Deposit on drink containers	Modal verbs	38 - 39
20	Discussion	The green thing	Writing the time	40 - 41
21	Graphics	Evolution	Dashes	42 - 43
22	Procedure	Making a Storyboard?	Hyphens (-)	44 - 45
23	Narrative	Cannibals' Gold	*And* after a comma	46 - 47
24	Biography	Spencer Williams	Small words from big words	48 - 49
25	Comic cover	Spider-man Comic covers	The prefix *super*	50 -51
26	Report	Cobbold Gorge	Spoonerisms	52 - 53
27	Explanation	Burial Styles	The suffix *ism*	54 - 55
28	Discussion	Effects of Media Violence	*i.e.* or *e.g.*?	56 - 57
29	Article	Natural Gemstones, Unnatural Names	People from other worlds	58 - 59
30	Narrative	Centrepoint	Comparative adjectives	60 - 61
31	Instruction	How to play quoits	*made from* OR *made of*	62 - 63
32	Poetry	Cormorant	How to use *etc.*	64 - 65
33	Procedure	Coal and Coal Seam Gas	The suffix *cide*	66 - 67
34	Report	One Touch could be Fatal	When to use an asterisk (*)	68 - 69
35	Narrative	Glenridge Bargain	Compound nouns	70 - 71
36	Description	The Lighthouse	Compound verbs	72 - 73
37	Explanation	Avenue of Honour	Words from Mars	74 - 75
38	Film review	Last Cab to Darwin	Compound adjectives	76 - 77
39	Recount	Discovery of Fairy Rings in Australia	*High* OR *tall*?	78 - 79
40	Eulogy	Sir Edmund Hillary	Word oddities	80 - 81

Understanding Year 8 Comprehension
A. Horsfield © Five Senses Education © W. Marlin

Bennelong

In November 1789 Bennelong (1764?–1813), a member of the Wangal clan, and Colebee, a Cadigal man, were kidnapped while they were fishing at Manly Cove. Governor Arthur Phillip (1738–1814) hoped that he would be able to learn the local Eora language and come to understand their culture and way of life. Despite being kept in chains for many weeks, Bennelong was invited to Government House as a guest. Colebee escaped but Bennelong stayed longer with Governor Phillip in his house and developed a close friendship with him.

Bennelong called Phillip 'Beanga', meaning father in the Eora language, and Phillip in return called him 'Durung', meaning son. When accompanying the governor, Bennelong learnt English, and adopted some of the values and attitudes of the British. Bennelong did escape but returned with some of his family and they made the yard at Government House their home. In 1791 Governor Phillip built a brick hut for Bennelong on the site of Djubuguli. The area became known as Bennelong Point. He played an important role as a mediator between the Aboriginal clans and the colonists.

In 1792 Bennelong and an Aboriginal youth, Yemmerrawanie, travelled with Governor Arthur Phillip to England. They were received by King George III in May 1793. Yemmerrawanie died in Britain and Bennelong's health became <u>precarious</u> because of the cold, homesickness and his disappointment in the long delay in returning to the colony. He arrived home in September 1795 with Governor John Hunter (1737–1821). Bennelong found that his hut had been demolished and his wife, Barangaroo, had left him. He had embraced many English customs and attitudes while he was away and found it difficult to return to his people. Before long Bennelong lost the respect of his people, the Eora, and without Phillip for support he had no status in the colony either. He died on 3 January 1813 and was buried at Kissing Point on the banks of the Parramatta River.

On their arrival, the British claimed the country as their own through the law of *terra nullius* (meaning land belonging to no-one) giving the local Indigenous people no rights to a treaty or any ownership of their land. By 1795 colonists had claimed the land of the Cadigal clan and neighbouring Aboriginal language groups, dislocating them from their own countries. This area was known as Wuganmagulya and is now occupied by the New South Wales Royal Botanical Gardens. The site is culturally and spiritually significant as it contains a Bora ring, a place where Aboriginal communities traditionally came together to hold initiation ceremonies. In 1795, the officers of the First Fleet, including David Collins (1756–1810), observed initiation ceremonies at this sacred place.

The Sydney Opera House now stands on the little point of land where Bennelong's house once stood.

Adapted from: http://www.myplace.edu.au/decades_timeline/1790/decade_landing_21.html?tabRank=2&subTabRank=2

Understanding recounts

Circle a letter to answer questions 1 to 8.

1. What happened to Bennelong's brick house?
    - A   it was allowed to fall into disrepair
    - B   it was rebuilt as the Royal Botanical Gardens
    - C   it was demolished in his absence
    - D   it was retained in the yard of Government House

2. Phillip's attitude to the kidnapping of the fishermen at Manly could be described as
    - A   an attempt to gain knowledge of the indigenous people
    - B   an act of premeditated cruelty
    - C   a chance to intimidate the local tribespeople
    - D   a thoughtless act of racial discrimination

3. You are told that: *Bennelong's health became precarious*
    As used in the text what does *precarious* mean?
    - A   precipitous
    - B   likely to fail
    - C   substantial
    - D   subject to threats

4. Bennelong's life could best be described as
    - A   being trapped between two cultures
    - B   a series of unexpected fortunate experiences
    - C   representing the improving relationship between two cultures
    - D   a journey from respect to entitlement

5. The area known as Wuganmagulya is significant because it is
    - A   the setting for Bennelong's burial place
    - B   where Governor Phillip first made contact with the Aboriginal people
    - C   the site where a treaty was signed with the traditional landowners
    - D   a place where Aboriginal communities met to perform ceremonies

6. What was the fate of Colebee?
    - A   he was left in England
    - B   he escaped from captivity
    - C   he died while in chains
    - D   he was integrated into the colony

7. In which year did Bennelong return from England?
    - A   1791
    - B   1792
    - C   1793
    - D   1795

8. The treatment of the indigenous people by the first settlers could best be described as
    - A   indifferent
    - B   fraudulent
    - C   compassionate
    - D   callous

Lit Tip 1 – Improve your Literacy skills   Life dates

A person's date of birth and demise can be shown in brackets after the person's name:

Governor John Hunter (1737–1821)

Bennelong's birth year was unknown. In the text his life is represented as (1764?–1813).

Circa (shortened to c.) is a more common device to show that an exact year is not known.
- c. 1732 – 1799: the end year is known accurately; the start year is approximate.
- 1732 – c. 1799: the start year is known accurately: the end year is approximate.
- c. 1732 – c. 1799: both years are approximate.

If the person is still alive it may be shown as Phil Chance (1998 –)

Understanding Year 8 Comprehension
A. Horsfield © Five Senses Education © W. Marlin

2 Read the procedure for *Life jackets.*

Life jackets

On planes life jackets are located either under your seat or under the centre armrest. Although most aircraft are fitted with life jackets, some airlines use passenger seat cushions as flotation devices rather than life jackets. The life jacket safety consideration may be excluded from the briefing if the aircraft flight path does not travel over or near large masses of water (Wikipedia, 2009).

- **Cabin crew will supply life jackets for infants**
- **In an emergency:**
  Remove the life jacket from any packaging
  Put the life jacket over your head
  Tie or clip straps together tightly around your waist
- **Do not inflate your life jacket until exiting the aircraft**
- **Inflate your life jacket by pulling down on the toggle**
  If the life jacket does not fully inflate after pulling down on the toggle, blow into the mouthpiece to inflate manually
  The torch light and whistle attached to the life jacket may be used for attracting attention

- **Always follow crew members' instructions and <u>comply with lighted signs</u> and posted placards on the aircraft**

Do not take any personal luggage with you when exiting the aircraft in an emergency.

These are general instructions. Remember, all aircraft differ in some way.

Review the aircraft safety card often held in the seat pocket in front of you. This will provide clarification of points mentioned during the pre-flight safety briefing as well as any additional safety information. For example, the aircraft safety card may cover operation of exits, the brace position, the use of life jackets and the use of oxygen masks.

Source: http://aviationknowledge.wikidot.com/aviation1:passenger-briefings

Understanding procedures   Circle a letter or write an answer for questions 1 to 8.

1. What is the value of the series of pictures?
   A   pictures are more appealing than text
   B   pictures provide a welcome diversion for passengers
   C   pictures are a more readily accessible set of steps than text
   D   pictures take up less page space than text

2. Life jacket information may **NOT** be included in a pre-flight briefing if
   A   the flight is not over a large area of water
   B   there are no infants on the flight
   C   insufficient life jackets are available
   D   the plane is a small plane with few passengers

3. In dot point 2 (**In an emergency**) you are told to *Put the life jacket over your head.*

   Which picture corresponds with this instruction? Write a number in the box. ☐

4. Passengers are requested to *comply* with lighted signs.
   Which would be an appropriate synonym for *comply* as used in the text.
   A   complete   B   bypass   C   confer   D   obey

5. According to the text which statement is TRUE?
   A   On all planes life jackets are kept under the seats.
   B   The aircraft safety card includes the same information as given by crew members.
   C   Pre-flight safety information is repeated regularly throughout the flight.
   D   On leaving a plane in an emergency passengers should only take essential items.

6. Passengers are advised to inflate their life jackets
   A   as soon as they are secured on the body
   B   once the passengers are in open water
   C   as they leave the aircraft
   D   when crew members give the okay

7. Which word from the text means: *press firmly against something to stay balanced*
   A   supply   B   inflate   C   held   D   brace

8. Other than life jackets what other devices are provided in an emergency evacuation?
   A   torch lights   B   placards
   C   seat cushions   D   oxygen masks

Lit Tip 2 – Improve your Literacy skills   *Colloquialisms or idioms*

A **colloquialism** is a group of words that is used in familiar conversation. They are not used commonly in formal or technical writing. I <u>wanna</u> get my <u>budgie</u> back.
Colloquial expression in speech in a narrative can give insights into a person's character.

An **Idiom** is a group of words, as established by usage, as having a meaning not obvious by the context. Olivia was <u>over the moon</u> with her results. Used wisely idiom can make language in text more colourful.

Tick the boxes for expressions that use idiom.

1. I am as sick as a dog. ☐   **2.** I ain't going home. ☐   **3.** Arnie was full of agro. ☐

4. We didn't go. It was raining cats and dogs. ☐   **5.** His win was out of the blue. ☐

Remember you do not need inverted commas around these expressions in writing.

Understanding Year 8 Comprehension
A. Horsfield © Five Senses Education © W. Marlin

3 Read the description of *Coketown.*

Hard Times was Dickens' tenth novel. It was first published in installments that began in April of 1854 and ran through August of that year.

Coketown

It was a town of red brick, or of brick that would have been red if the smoke and ashes had allowed it; but as matters stood, it was a town of unnatural red and black like the painted face of a savage. It was a town of machinery and tall chimneys, out of which interminable serpents of smoke trailed themselves for ever and ever, and never got uncoiled. It had a black canal in it, and a river that ran purple with ill-smelling dye, and vast piles of buildings full of windows where there was a rattling and a trembling all day long, and where the piston of the steam-engine worked monotonously up and down, like the head of an elephant in a state of melancholy madness.

HARD TIMES.

BOOK THE FIRST. SOWING.

It contained several large streets all very like one another, and many small streets still more like one another, inhabited by people equally like one another, who all went in and out at the same hours, with the same sound upon the same pavements, to do the same work, and to whom every day was the same as yesterday and tomorrow, and every year the counterpart of the last and the next.

You saw nothing in Coketown but what was severely workful. If the members of a religious persuasion built a chapel there, they made it a pious warehouse of red brick with a bell in a bird cage on top of it.

All the public inscriptions in the town were painted alike, in severe _____(5)_____ of black and white. The jail might have been the infirmary, the infirmary might have been the jail, the town-hall might have been either, or both, or anything else, for anything that appeared to the contrary in the graces of their construction. Fact, fact, fact, everywhere in the material aspect of the town; fact, fact, fact, everywhere in the immaterial. The M'Choakum child school was all fact, and the school of design was all fact, and the relations between master and man were all fact, and everything was fact between the lying-in hospital and the cemetery, and what you couldn't state in figures, or show to be purchaseable in the cheapest market and saleable in the dearest, was not, and never should be, world without end, Amen.

Adapted from Hard Times by Charles Dickens
http://www.charlesdickensinfo.com/novels/hard-times/

Understanding descriptions

Circle a letter to answer questions 1 to 8.

1. The writer describes the chapel in Coketown as a *pious warehouse*.
   When he says this he is being

   A   sarcastic   B   facetious   C   belittling   D   boorish

2. The most likely reason the writer concludes the text with Amen is because

   A   it underpins his empathy for the working class
   B   it shows due respect for the Coketown religious leaders
   C   he sees this as the way things are and how they will remain
   D   there is no respite for the people of Coketown

3. What aspect of Coketown made a deep impression on the writer?

   A   the extensive devastation of the environment
   B   the diligence of townsfolk towards their workplace
   C   the vibrant industry of the factories
   D   the unavoidable sameness of everything

4. Which of these quotes from the text is a metaphor?

   A   like the painted face of a savage
   B   serpents of smoke trailed themselves for ever and ever,
   C   a river that ran purple with ill-smelling dye
   D   like the head of an elephant in a state of melancholy madness.

5. A word has been deleted from the text. Which word would be best suited to the space (5)?

   A   colours   B   warnings
   C   shapes   D   characters

6. In the text the writer comments on the

   A   importance of having gainful employment
   B   need for standardisation in signage
   C   monotonous grind of factory life
   D   industriousness of Coketown folk

7. What is the main focus of the first paragraph?

   A   the reason for the canal's state   B   a description of town buildings
   C   working conditions in factories   D   the unrelenting industrial noise

8. The novel, *Hard Times*, can be described as a historical novel.
   Which of the following statements would **NOT** apply to a historical novel?

   A   Historical novels focus primarily on reporting accurately historical facts.
   B   Historical novels use history to deliver plausible storylines.
   C   Historical novels bring significant past events and people's lifestyles to life.
   D   Historical novels help readers reflect on present day circumstances.

Lit Tip 3 – Improve your Literacy skills   **Writing descriptions**

A descriptive text is a text that wants you to picture what is being described. In a novel you might *imagine* the characters. In a travel book you might *visualise* a setting.

Descriptive texts make use of adjectives and adverbs, use comparisons and engage the reader's five senses.

Underline the adverbs and highlight the adjectives in this sentence: The early dawn air was crisp and sharp as bright sunlight boldly caught the white peaks.

Understanding Year 8 Comprehension
A. Horsfield © Five Senses Education © W. Marlin

The Theia Hypothesis

New evidence emerges that the Earth and the Moon were part of the same celestial body. According to the giant impact hypothesis, there was once a Mars-sized body referred to as Theia orbiting in our solar system. The planet was named after the Greek Titan who gave birth to the Moon goddess Selene - a fitting name considering that the planet Theia is thought to be responsible for the birth of our moon.

Theia would have formed in about the same orbit as Earth, but about 60° ahead or behind. When the protoplanet had grown to be about the size of Mars, its size made it too heavy for its orbit to remain stable. As a result, its angular distance from Earth varied increasingly, until it finally crashed into the Earth.

The collision would have occurred circa 4.533 billion years ago when Theia would have hit the Earth at an oblique angle, and destroyed herself in the process. Theia's mantle and a significant portion of the Earth's silicate mantle were thrust into space. The left over materials from Theia mixed with the materials from the Earth and eventually formed the Moon.

New research is validating this hypothesis, showing that the Earth's core and the Moon's core contain the same silicon isotopic material, which would support that the two were once a single body until a large impact separated them.

Scientists compared silicon isotopes from Earth rocks, as well as other materials from our solar system such as rocky materials from meteorites.

Up to about 2,900 kilometres into the Earth (not quite half way to the centre), is what we know as the mantle and crust. They are predominantly formed of silicate, a compound made of silicon, oxygen, and other elements. Past the halfway mark is a dense metallic iron material that makes up the Earth's core.

A multinational team found that the heavier isotopes from silicate samples taken from the Earth consisted of increased amounts of the heavier isotopes of silicon. They found that Mars, the asteroid Vesta, and various chondrites (primitive meteorites) do not contain such an arrangement, even though they have an iron core which is much smaller than the Earth (about one-eighth the size), so did not have enough mass to generate the pressure necessary to form the same core as found in the Earth.

However, such a core does exist at the centre of the Moon, but no one can explain how it got there.

Adapted from: http://www.dailygalaxy.com/my_weblog/2007/07/the-theia-hypot.html

Understanding information reports

Circle a letter to answer questions 1 to 8.

1. The text could be described as
   - A an exposition
   - B a factual recount
   - C a fictional description
   - D an information report

2. What was the name of the solar body that was once thought to be in the same orbit as the Earth?
   - A Titan
   - B Vesta
   - C Theia
   - D Selene

3. The article, *The Theia Hypothesis*, would be most suitable in a magazine featuring
   - A astrology
   - B astronomy
   - C aerodynamics
   - D archaeology

4. The theory that the Earth and its moon may have been part of the same body is validated by the fact
   - A they are both part of the same solar system
   - B of their relatively close proximity to one another
   - C the moon's angular distance from Earth remains constant
   - D the core of each contains the same silicon isotopic material

5. What is made up mainly of a compound of silicon, oxygen, and other elements?
   - A the Earth's core
   - B rocky materials from meteorites
   - C the mantle and crust of the Earth
   - D the moon's core

6. Which was the fate of Theia?
   - A it disintegrated to form asteroids and meteorites
   - B it broke away from Earth to became our moon
   - C it was consumed by the Earth's core
   - D it was destroyed on impact with Earth

7. What is thought to have prevented the cores of Mars, the Vesta asteroid, and some meteorites from forming Earth-like cores?
   - A the mass of the iron core
   - B the lack of a solar collision
   - C the absence of silicon
   - D the distance from the sun

8. An hypothesis is
   - A an idea that may be true on the basis of speculation
   - B a proposed explanation based on limited evidence
   - C a proposition that is open to dispute based on scientific evidence
   - D a statement from which an inference can be made

Lit Tip 4 – Improve your Literacy skills　　　　　*Majority* – correct usage

Q. Is *majority* a singular noun or a plural noun?

A. *Majority* may be used as either singular or plural, depending upon context. When used to describe a collective group it is singular. When it is used for a collection of individuals, it is plural.

Example 1. The majority of senators elects the leader. (singular with the verb elects)
Example 2. The majority of politicians vote thoughtfully. (plural with the verb vote)

Look at this sentence. The majority of train stations are unattended.

Is *majority* singular or plural? Highlight your response.

Source: http://www.word-mart.com/html/word_usage_tips.html#Majority

Understanding Year 8 Comprehension
A. Horsfield © Five Senses Education © W. Marlin

Memory

Late, late last night, when the whole world slept,
Along to the garden of dreams I crept.
And I pulled the bell of an old, old house
Where the moon dipped down like a little white mouse.

I tapped the door and I tossed my head:
"Are you in, little girl? Are you in?" I said.
And while I waited and shook with cold
Through the door tripped me - just eight years old.

I looked so sweet with my pigtails down,
Tied up with a ribbon of dusky brown,
With a dimpled chin full of childish charm,
And my old black dolly asleep in my arms.

I sat me down when I saw myself,
And I told little tales of a moonland elf.
I laughed and sang as I used to do
When the world was ruled by Little Boy Blue.

Then I danced with a toss and a twirl
And said: "Now have you been a good, good girl?
Have you had much spanking since you were Me?
And does it feel fine to be twenty-three?"

I kissed me then, and I said farewell,
For I've earned more spanks than I dared to tell,
And Eight must never see Twenty-three
As she peeps through the door of Memory.

Zora Bernice May Cross (1890—1964)

Zora Bernice May Cross was an Australian poet, novelist and journalist.
She was born in Brisbane, and was educated at Ipswich Girls' Grammar School and then Sydney
Teachers' College. She taught for three years and then worked as a journalist, for the *Boomerang* and
then as a freelance writer.

Understanding poetry

Circle a letter to answer questions 1 to 8.

1. Who did the narrator meet in the 'garden of dreams'?
   A her childhood self
   B a neighbour's child
   C her childhood friend
   D a make-believe friend

2. The poem evokes feelings of
   A reflectiveness
   B nostalgia
   C regret
   D contemplation

3. The poet uses a number of literary devices. She has **NOT** used
   A alliteration
   B repetition
   C similes
   D hyperboles

4. Where did the meeting between the main characters actually take place?
   A in a bedroom
   B at a cottage door
   C in a dream
   D within a garden

5. What is implied by the line: When the world was ruled by Little Boy Blue?
   A children cannot separate fact from fantasy
   B Little Boy Blue was a bully
   C childhood is a time of innocence
   D imaginary friendships should be discarded

6. From information in the poem which option best describes the character of the narrator?
   A tranquil
   B unruly
   C solemn
   D nonchalant

7. The line in Stanza 8 has: Eight must never see Twenty-three uses capital letters for numbers. What is the likely reason for this?
   A it is a convention of early last century
   B they are intended to be exact numbers
   C to emphasise the age difference
   D the numbers replace proper names

8. In stanza 6 the narrator does not answer the question posed in stanza 5: does it feel fine to be twenty-three?
   The most likely reason for this is that
   A the narrator does not know the answer
   B no one can know what their future holds
   C the narrator can only give a negative answer
   D there was no time for the answer

Lit Tip 5 – Improve your Literacy skills   **The suffix _arian_**

The suffix _arian_ refers to a person who has a particular characteristic or feature.
Examples: vegetarian, librarian, disciplinarian, barbarian, parliamentarian

What is a person called: who rules with strict authority? _____

who is a century old? _____(Take care with the spelling)

who is an expert in grammar? _____

Two similar suffixes
The suffix _arium_ (or ariom) refers to a place. **Examples:** aquarium, terrarium

What is a place called where planets are observed? _____

Understanding Year 8 Comprehension
A. Horsfield © Five Senses Education © W. Marlin

Gympie-Gympie stinging tree

North Queensland road surveyor A.C. Macmillan was among the first to document the effects of a stinging tree, reporting to his boss in 1866 that his packhorse "was stung, got mad, and died within two hours". Similar tales abound in local folklore of horses jumping in agony off cliffs and forestry workers drinking themselves silly to dull the intractable pain.

Writing to Marina in 1994, Australian ex-serviceman Cyril Bromley described falling into a stinging tree during military training on the tablelands in World War II. Strapped to a hospital bed for three weeks and administered all manner of unsuccessful treatments, he was sent "as mad as a cut snake" by the pain. Cyril also told of an officer shooting himself after using a stinging-tree leaf for "toilet purposes".

He's had too many stings to count but Ernie Rider will never forget the day in 1963 that he was slapped in the face, arms and chest by a stinging tree. "I remember it feeling like there were giant hands trying to squash my chest," he said. "For two or three days the pain was almost unbearable; I couldn't work or sleep, then it was pretty bad pain for another fortnight or so. The stinging persisted for two years and recurred every time I had a cold shower."

Now a senior conservation officer with the Queensland Parks and Wildlife Service, Ernie said he's not experienced anything like the pain during 44 year's work in the bush. "There's nothing to rival it; it's 10 times worse than anything else – scrub ticks, scrub itch and itchy-jack sting included. Stinging trees are a real and present danger."

Gympie-Gympie: stings like acid
So swollen was Les Moore after being stung across the face several years ago that he said he resembled Mr Potato Head.

"I think I went into anaphylactic shock and it took days for my sight to recover," said Les, a scientific officer with the CSIRO Division of Wildlife and Ecology in Queensland, who was near Bartle Frere (North Peak) studying cassowaries when disaster struck. "Within minutes the initial stinging and burning intensified and the pain in my eyes was like someone had poured acid on them. My mouth and tongue swelled up so much that I had trouble breathing. It was debilitating and I had to blunder my way out of the bush."

It was perhaps this rapid and savage reaction that inspired the British Army's interest in the more sinister applications of the Gympie-Gympie stinging tree in 1968. That year, the Chemical Defence Establishment at Porton Down (a top-secret laboratory that developed chemical weapons) contracted Alan Seawright, then a Professor of Pathology at the University of Queensland, to dispatch stinging-tree specimens.

"Chemical warfare is their work, so I could only assume that they were investigating its potential as a biological weapon," said Alan. Alan became an honorary research consultant (1991 - 94) to the University of Queensland's National Research Centre in Environmental Toxicology. "I never heard anything more, so I guess we'll never know."

Sources: Australian Geographic Apr - Jun 2008
http://www.australiangeographic.com.au/topics/science-environment/2009/06/gympie-gymp-ie-once-stung,-never-forgotten, http://blog.neilennis.com/index.php/the-bump-track/

Understanding recounts

Circle a letter or write an answer for questions 1 to 8.

1. The effects of contact with the Gympie-Gympie stinging tree could best be described as
   A fatal with a delayed reaction
   B excruciating with a sudden onset
   C wildly fluctuating but rapidly abating
   D agonising but short lived

2. Who was strapped to a bed for three weeks after coming in contact with the stinging tree?
   Write your answer on the line. _____

3. In paragraph 5 Les Moore says *he resembled Mr Potato Head*.
   The expression *he resembled Mr Potato Head* is an example of
   A an analogy   B a simile
   C a metaphor   D an acronym

4. In which order did the events in the text occur?
   1. British Army develops an interest in the stinging tree
   2. a packhorse was stung, went mad, and died within two hours
   3. a scientific officer lost his sight when he encountered the stinging tree
   4. an ex-serviceman fell into a stinging tree during military training

   A **3, 2, 1, 4**   B **2, 4, 3, 1**   C **2, 3, 1, 4**   D **2, 3, 4, 1**

5. In the text, the first person to document the afflictions caused by the stinging tree was
   A a surveyor   B an ex-serviceman
   C a forestry worker   D a conservation officer

6. What is the most likely reason the writer describes the British Army's interest in the stinging tree as sinister (paragraph 7)?
   A they refused to acknowledge the suffering of early victims
   B they had little regard for contract collectors in the region
   C they couldn't comprehend the distress the sting caused living creatures
   D they may have had intentions of using the toxins on humans

7. The use of the term *toilet purposes* in paragraph 2 is an example of
   A a hyperbole   B a colloquialism
   C a euphemism   D an analogy

8. What was the most extreme reaction by a person stung by the stinging tree?
   A riding a horse over a cliff
   B going into anaphylactic shock
   C drinking themselves silly to dull the pain
   D committing suicide with a gun shot

Lit Tip 6 – Improve your Literacy skills   **The prefix *auto***

Auto has more than one meaning. Look at these examples. Add examples of your own.
   1. self-propelling (automobile), _____
   2. by oneself (autobiography), _____
   3. spontaneous (automatic) _____

What is an automat? _____

Understanding Year 8 Comprehension
A. Horsfield © Five Senses Education © W. Marlin

7 Read the book review 'The Adventures of Scrounger the Tortoise Shell Cat and Charlie the Tortoise with a tortoise shell,' by R.G.Weavers.

The Adventures of Scrounger the Tortoise Shell Cat and Charlie the Tortoise with a tortoise shell

This is the story of two, much loved, pets who arrive from the UK to live in Australia with their family. Their owners, the Wetherall family, have emigrated to Australia after buying a sugar cane farm and cattle station in the far north of Queensland.

From the very first night, after they are released from quarantine, Scrounger the Tortoise Shell Cat and Charlie the Tortoise discover that although Australia is undoubtedly a land of adventure, none of their adventures will be quite the same as they experienced in England!

Whilst the family settle into their first year of farming, their children, Sammie and Adam and their pets, Charlie and Scrounger have a whole stream of unexpected and exciting adventures around the farm and the surrounding bushlands.

Old Nugget, the Wetherall Station Aboriginal Head Stockman takes the children and their pets under his wing. He teaches them how to recognise friend from foe and live safely amongst the diversity of animals and surrounding habitat.

He even lets Scrounger in on his big secret!

New friends come in all shapes and sizes from Gumbo the goanna to Grinchy, the grouchy blue tongued lizard and certainly their biggest mates to date, the massive water buffaloes, Wally and his Missus.

Scrounger gets on the wrong side of a taipan, the world's most venomous snake, but manages to go from deadly enemies to best of mates.

The farm year ends with everyone on the Station celebrating their hard work by banding together in the Wetherall Farm Cricket team to battle for, _The Ashes_, against their predecessor's traditional <u>arch</u>-rivals, the Gloucester Farm from up in the Tablelands, at the annual Cricket Festival. And what a day it turns out to be!

This fascinating saga of Charlie and Scrounger in Australia is a non-stop journey of excitement, surprise, danger, sadness and laughter, but always a fun-filled and action packed adventure.

Charlie the Tortoise, never says a lot but even Scrounger agrees when Charlie sums up their first year in Australia, when he quietly declares, "Best Ever!"

We think you will agree!

Our thanks to Roy Weavers for permission to reproduce this review.
First published in PORT DOUGLAS in Newsport Corporation Summer edition 2016
Available at store@mossmanprint.com.au

Understanding book reviews   Circle a letter or write an answer for questions 1 to 8.

1. Scrounger and Charlie found life on the farm to be an unexpected experience because they
    A   had spent their lives in quarantine
    B   felt threatened most of the time
    C   came from a place that was totally different
    D   were not used to farm animals

2. Old Nugget has a secret (paragraph 5). The reviewer does not reveal what it is. Why?
    A   to encourage people to purchase and read the book
    B   the secret is not revealed in the book
    C   the reviewer has not read the whole book
    D   it's against old Nugget's custom to disclose secrets

3. This review could be regarded as a
    A   guarded review   B   persuasive review
    C   verbose review   D   cautious review

4. Which is the reason the words *The Ashes* (paragraph 8) are in italics?
    A   to draw the reader's attention to the particular words
    B   it's the title of a cricketing publication
    C   to give great importance to the winner of the match
    D   it's the name of a very specific and famous trophy

5. *Arch* (paragraph 8) is used to describe the rival team.
   In this context the prefix *arch* means
    A   unbending   B   unbeatable   C   chief   D   cunning

6. Which word from the text means a long story of heroic achievement?
    A   saga   B   diversity   C   journey   D   adventure

7. Which animal does the text suggest was the most dangerous for Scrounger and Charlie?
    A   the water buffaloes   B   the taipan snake
    C   the blue tongued lizard   D   the goanna

8. Name one animal whose name incorporates alliteration._____

Lit Tip 7 – Improve your Literacy skills   **Using italics**

The purpose of italics is to aid the reader's comprehension of text by separating words and phrases from surrounding text. Most often italics are used for -
   • emphasis so that a word or phrase gets noticed
   • foreign words that have not been been integrated into English
   • the titles of books, magazines and other publications
   • scientific names
   • the titles of broadcast material and events
The title of works **NOT** italicised include religious books (**e.g.** Bible, Koran, Torah).

Read this sentence aloud to see how italics can modify the meaning.
   1. I read *your* story but I didn't enjoy it.   **2.** I read your story but *I* didn't enjoy it.

Understanding Year 8 Comprehension
A. Horsfield © Five Senses Education © W. Marlin

The coconut tree legend

The coconut tree is one of the most common trees in the Tahitian islands. The Polynesians of Tahiti always tell a legend about its creation.

A long time ago, a young girl called Hina was of real beauty due to her sun kissed skin and silky hair. She was meant to marry the Prince of Eels. Frightened by the _____(4)_____ of her suitor, who had a gigantic body and an enormous head, Hina ran away and took refuge in the house of the fishing God – Hiro.

Photo A. Horsfield

The latter was dazzled by the beauty of Hina and touched by her history, so he took one of the young woman's hairs and with it he fished the approaching eel. Hiro cut up the prince of eels and wrapped his head in leaves. Before dying, the eel said to Hina, "Of all the people who hate me, including you Hina, you will one day kiss me to thank me. I will die, but my <u>prediction is eternal.</u>"

Hiro entrusted the head of the eel to Hina and then advised her, 'Hina, girl of beauty, you can return to your family and there, you will destroy this head. But throughout your journey do not put it on the ground because then the curse of the eel will come true.'

On her way back, the beautiful young woman and her followers who accompanied her, became tired and decided to bathe in the river, forgetting the warning of the God Hiro. The eel's head which had been put on the ground penetrated the earth, and from it a large tree was born, with a long trunk just like an immense eel, and with foliage similar to hair. The coconut tree had just been born!

Hina was then condemned by the Gods to remain close to this river because the tree had become taboo. Life went on until the day when a terrible dryness struck the lands and during which only the coconut resisted the sun. Thus, in spite of the God's prohibition to touch this tree, men picked its fruit full of clear and nutritive water.

Each fruit was marked with three dark spots laid out like two eyes and a mouth on which the men put their lips in order to drink the coconut water. Hina did the same thing - and the prophecy of the Prince of Eels had just come true.

Sources: http://tnt.pa-tahiti-tourplan.com/guide-2/polynesian-legends/the-coconut-tree-legend/

Understanding legends

Circle a letter or write an answer for questions 1 to 8.

1. The purpose of this legend is to
   - A explain a natural phenomenon
   - B extol the virtues of a heroic person
   - C provide a moral lesson
   - D foretell the consequences of an action

2. Which prediction did the eel make for Hina?
   - A Hina would not return to her village
   - B Hina would one day kiss the eel
   - C Hina would not taste the coconut's nutritious water
   - D Hina would spend her life in a river

3. An eternal prediction (paragraph 2) is a prediction that
   - A is given from the heart
   - B has no obligations
   - C is not restricted to any person
   - D lasts forever

4. A word has been deleted from the text.
   Which word would be best suited to the space (4)?
   - A charm
   - B proximity
   - C physique
   - D age

5. Write the numbers 1 to 4 in the boxes to show the correct order in which events occurred in the legend. The first one (1) has been done for you.

	Hiro cuts off the head of the Prince of Eels
	the land becomes dry and parched
	Hina and her companions decide to bathe in a river
1	Hina escapes her marriage with the Prince of Eels

6. The eel's head was put on the ground
   - A because Hina forgot the warning she had been given
   - B to fulfil the wishes of Hiro
   - C because the eel needed to return to the river
   - D to allow a coconut tree to develop

7. Which word from the text is the opposite to *former*? _____

8. According to the text what is unusual about the coconut?
   - A the trees near rivers remain taboo
   - B the coconut fruit looks like the head of an eel
   - C kissing a coconut will bring misfortune
   - D the foliage looks like a head of hair

Lit Tip 8 – Improve your Literacy skills   **Use of *former* and *latter***

Did you find Q.7 difficult?

Traditionally, **former** and **latter** are used in relation to pairs of items: either the first of two items (**former**) or the second of two items (**latter**). The reason for this is that **former** and **latter** were formed as comparative adjectives, and comparatives are correctly used with reference to just two things. Comparative adjectives often end with er.

Superlative adjectives are used where there are more than two things – the long**est** library book.

Underline the best word to complete this sentence.

   Bill was older than John but the (latter, former) was one year ahead at school.

Understanding Year 8 Comprehension
A. Horsfield © Five Senses Education © W. Marlin

Are green potatoes safe?

The potato make-up

The role of a potato tuber for the potato plant is to produce the next generation of potatoes. It contains nutrients in the form of starches, sugars, proteins and minerals for the new potato plant.

When a tuber is exposed to light it turns green by producing chlorophyll. It then makes extra energy for a new plant through photosynthesis. The green patches act in the same way as leaves.

The potato plant has the ability to produce its own protective chemicals which can make it lethal to insects, animals and fungi. These protective chemicals (glycoalkaloids) are at high levels in the leaves, stems and sprouts, (often called eyes) of the potato plant but are normally at very low levels in potato tubers.

Upon exposure to light the potato tuber will produce elevated levels of these protective glycoalkaloids, with the highest levels being in the sprouts as they emerge from the tuber.

Potatoes will also produce high levels of glycoalkaloids in response to bruising, cutting and other forms of physical damage, as well as to rotting caused by fungi or bacteria. In these instances high levels of glycoalkaloids are present in the potato. However, in non-damaged potatoes, greening is a warning sign. Some undiagnosed cases of gastroenteritis have been caused by eating green potatoes.

Are green potatoes safe to eat?

Green potatoes may cause food poisoning and since some of the symptoms are similar to gastroenteritis it is possible that some undiagnosed cases of gastroenteritis (vomiting and diarrhoea) have been caused by eating green potatoes.

Human and livestock deaths have been recorded from eating greened or damaged potatoes with very high levels. It should be noted that these are not destroyed by cooking, even by frying in hot oil. Consequently, potatoes with pronounced greening or with signs of damage should not be eaten.

_____(8)_____

Not every potato with traces of greening will contain sufficient levels of glycoalkaloids to pose a health threat. Because of the possibility that green potatoes may produce food poisoning, they should be discarded, as should physically damaged potatoes and those with signs of rotting.

Consumers should avoid buying potatoes that show signs of greening or damage and should carefully remove any sprouts before cooking. Remember, healthy potatoes do not pose any health risk and are an excellent source of nutrients.

Adapted from: http://www.csiro.au/en/Outcomes/Food-and-Agriculture/green-potatoes.aspx

Understanding explanations

Circle a letter to answer questions 1 to 8.

1. What is the function of chlorophyll in a potato tuber?
    - A to show that the potato may be unsafe
    - B to provide energy for a new plant
    - C to produce lethal protective chemicals
    - D to protect the plant from predators

2. Which part of this potato is an eye?

3. The highest levels of glycoalkaloid are most often found in the potatoes'
    - A sprouts
    - B leaves
    - C stems
    - D leaf tips

4. When can the highest levels of glycoalkaloid develop in a potato?
    - A as the potato starts to rot
    - B after the potato has been physically damaged
    - C when the tuber has signs of bruising
    - D with new shoots as they emerge from the tuber

5. The word *generation*, as used in paragraph 1, refers to
    - A all the sprouts that develop at the same time
    - B the time it takes a tuber to form
    - C a new stage in the potatoes life cycle
    - D the production of energy for growth

6. The writer is adamant about the alarming dangers posed by green potatoes.

    Is this statement TRUE or FALSE? Tick a box. TRUE ☐ FALSE ☐

7. Glycoalkaloids in potatoes, at times, could be described as
    - A contagious
    - B malignant
    - C infectious
    - D toxic

8. A subheading has been deleted from the text.
    Which heading would be best suited to the space (8)?
    - A New evidence
    - B Conclusions
    - C How to discard potatoes
    - D Buying potatoes

Lit Tip 9 – Improve your Literacy skills **Starting sentences with *And***

And is a coordinating conjunction (along with *but* or *or*).
It is particularly useful to start a sentence with these conjunctions if you're aiming to create a dramatic or forceful effect. You are aiming to draw attention to a particular point.
Examples: An announcer may say, '*And* now we come to the highlight of the evening.'

Some people are calling this his worst game ever. *And* who are we to argue?

Warning: Don't overdo do it! Your text will become choppy.
They climbed to the top of the dune. **And** *then they had a rest.* **And** *ate their sandwiches.* X
It is unwise to use *And* (*But* or *Or*) as a sentence starter in formal writing.
But it is okay to start sentences with and *And* is if you have a good reason!

Understanding Year 8 Comprehension
A. Horsfield © Five Senses Education © W. Marlin

Applying for a Job

Most written job applications require a cover letter and a résumé.

Cover letters typically provides detailed information on why you are qualified for the job you are applying for. They explain the reasons for your interest in the specific position and identify your most relevant skills or experiences. A cover letter accompanies your résumé.

Your cover letter may make the difference between obtaining a job interview and having your résumé ignored. It is the first impression an employer gets of you, the applicant. First impressions are lasting impressions. It makes sense to devote the necessary time and effort to writing the cover letter. It is a critical way to bring attention to the résumé and to succinctly highlight your abilities to any potential employer. It is important to follow the employer's instructions on how to submit your application

Your résumé is a list of your credentials pertinent to the job you are seeking.
Your résumé should include;
- **Education:** standards reached, high schools attended, current studies or grades, relevant non-school qualifications
- **Any employment history** - this could be part-time or volunteer work
- **Achievements** - these may be educational, sporting and special interests
- **References** - usually two referees are required - and not relatives. Have written references from someone respected amongst your associations.

Wherever possible add documented evidence of qualifications, certificates, photographs or references along with your résumé. Photocopies only. Mislaid originals are difficult to replace.

Writing an effective job application, cover letter.
1. Take the time to target your cover letter to the actual position. This means customising any cover letter you write, so it specifically relates your skills to the job required.
2. State the reasons for your interest in the position.
3. State how you learned of the position and the title of the position you are applying for. This way the person reading your cover letter will know which job you are interested in.
4. Express your enthusiasm for the position.
5. Identify your most relevant skills and experiences, but don't just duplicate your resume. Highlight skills that most match the job.
6. Refer to the qualifications listed for the position and illustrate how your abilities relate.
7. Communicate your interest, motivation, and strengths. Emphasise your achievements.
8. Indicate how you can be contacted and thank the company for their consideration.
9. Review sample cover letters but do not copy them verbatim.
10. Avoid clichés and meaningless or wordy expressions – and spelling mistakes.

And, of course, it must be honest.

"Everything on your resume is true ... right?"

Adapted from: http://jobsearch.about.com/cs/coverletters/ht/coverletter.htm

Understanding applications

Circle a letter to answer questions 1 to 8.

1. What is a résumé?
   - A   an itemisation of your relevant credentials
   - B   a succinct and private autobiography
   - C   a record of important achievements in life
   - D   a detailed outline of one's interests

2. What does the writer suggest is the most important aspect of a cover letter?
   - A   the depth of credential details relevant to the advertised position
   - B   the manner in which it creates the employer's first impression
   - C   an absence of spelling mistakes and grammatical errors
   - D   an obvious eagerness for the getting paid work

3. What is meant by *verbatim* (point 9)?
   - A   spoken correctly
   - B   using unnecessary words
   - C   word for word
   - D   overuse of verbs

4. What is the relevance of beginning the last sentence with *And*? (Check out **Lit Tip 9**.)
   - A   it destroys the credibility of the article
   - B   it is an example of what not to do in an application
   - C   it indicates that it's a minor point that is being made
   - D   it is aiming to create a dramatic and forceful effect

5. Documented evidence supporting an application should be
   - A   attached to the cover letter
   - B   in a separate file
   - C   forwarded on request
   - D   with the résumé

6. Which of the following may **not** be detrimental when applying for a position of employment?
   - A   a commercially produced standardised cover letter
   - B   unsupported evidence of qualifications
   - C   a lack of previous permanent work experience
   - D   a cover letter taken directly from another source

7. The underlying theme of the article suggests that applicants for positions should be
   - A   forceful
   - B   courteous
   - C   grateful
   - D   solemn

8. What is suggested by the cartoon?
   - A   The interviewer doesn't believe the applicant.
   - B   The interviewer has not read the application.
   - C   The applicant has an unacceptable facial feature.
   - D   The applicant is not suitable for the position applied for.

Lit Tip 10 – Improve your Literacy skills   *Effect* or *affect*

Effect and *affect* are often incorrectly used because they sound much the same.
Affect can be a noun or a verb. Weather conditions will affect the attendance. (verb)
The son took his father's accident with little affect. (noun)
Effect can be used as a noun when talking about a result.
What was the effect of the loss on the team? *Effect* can follow *an* or *the*.

Underline the correct word.

   1. Your opinion will not (affect effect) my decision to leave.
   2. Transport costs have an (affect, effect) on prices.
   3. The cheap medicine had a disastrous (effect, affect) on his condition!

Understanding Year 8 Comprehension
A. Horsfield © Five Senses Education © W. Marlin

11 Look at the plan of the *Wind Spirit* layout.

Wind Spirit Layout

The Wind Spirit is a tourist yacht that operates in some of the world's best small ports and hidden harbors. It carries just 148 guests and operates out of Tahiti in the Society Islands in the South Pacific. Passengers' quarters are on Deck Two.
Staff quarters are on Deck One.

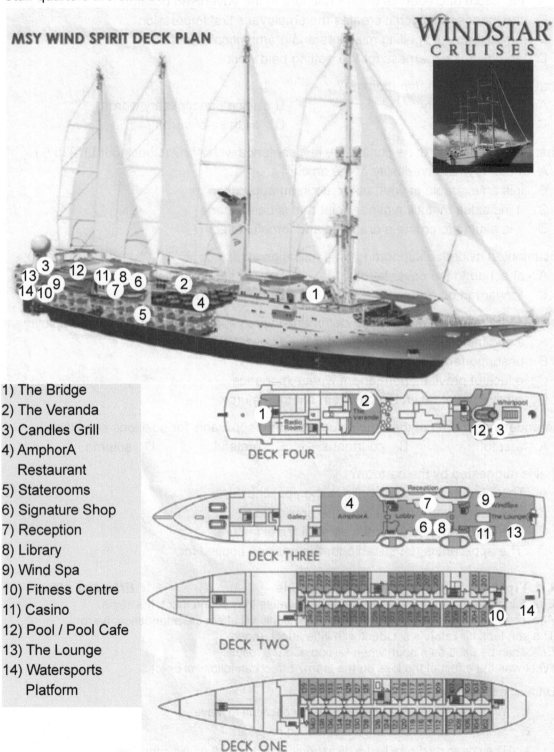

1) The Bridge
2) The Veranda
3) Candles Grill
4) AmphorA
   Restaurant
5) Staterooms
6) Signature Shop
7) Reception
8) Library
9) Wind Spa
10) Fitness Centre
11) Casino
12) Pool / Pool Cafe
13) The Lounge
14) Watersports
   Platform

Source: Information fact sheet provide on Wind Star

Understanding plans

Circle a letter to answer questions 1 to 8.

1. This plan would most likely be intended for
   A   the captain of the Wind Spirit
   B   passengers joining a cruise
   C   the vessel's maintenance crew
   D   the builders of Wind Spirit

2. The Fitness Centre is on the same deck as the
   A   water sports platform
   B   bridge
   C   Amphora restaurant
   D   library

3. To get from the staff quarters to the galley kitchen staff have to
   A   stay on the same deck but go towards the rear of the vessel
   B   proceed to the front of the vessel then climb to the next deck
   C   climb up two decks and head to the Amphora restaurant
   D   go down one deck and head to the sports platform

4. On which deck is the Signature Shop?
   A   Deck 1   B   Deck 2   C   Deck 3   D   Deck 4

5. Which word best describe the location of the bridge on the Wind Spirit?
   A   on the port side
   B   on the starboard
   C   at the aft of the vessel
   D   at the fore of the vessel

6. These are the life boats and shore boats.

   They are located
   A   beside the pool cafe
   B   next to the bridge
   C   under the veranda
   D   adjacent to the casino

7. A stateroom may also be called a
   A   bunk   B   cabin   C   unit   D   berth

8. According to the plan which statement is CORRECT?
   A   The library is above the passengers' quarters.
   B   The restaurant is more forward than the galley.
   C   The bridge is on the same deck as the fitness centre.
   D   The water sports platform is on the top deck (4).

Lit Tip 11 – Improve your Literacy skills   **Nautical terms**

These are some useful nautical (relating to navigation) terms.

   fore: to the front section of a vessel   **aft:** to the back section of a vessel
   stern: the back half of a vessel   **bow:** the front half of a vessel
   port: left side of a vessel going forward   **starboard:** the right side
   galley: a vessel's kitchen   **forecastle:** crew's living quarters
   bridge: the elevated operational centre where the captain directs operations

In nautical terms what is the opposite of **starboard**? _____, **aft**? _____

Now try **stern**: _____

Understanding Year 8 Comprehension
A. Horsfield © Five Senses Education © W. Marlin

Savannahlander Itinerary

Wednesday: Day 1 of a 4-day rail journey - Cairns to Almaden
6.30 am The Savannahlander departs Cairns station, located in Cairns Central Shopping Centre. Be at the station at least 15 minutes before departure. There is no food available at the station or on board the train so please organise breakfast at your accommodation or bring food to eat on the train.

If you would like to be picked up at Freshwater station let us know when booking.

7.30am We get a good look at the famous Stoney Creek Falls.

7.50am The train stops at Barron Falls station for a look at the mighty, cascading falls.

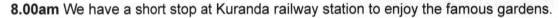

8.00am We have a short stop at Kuranda railway station to enjoy the famous gardens.

9.20am The train arrives in Mareeba and stops to set down and pick up passengers if required. Those doing the Barron River Rover trip have a short wait at Mareeba station for the bus back to Kuranda/Cairns.

10.10am The Savannahlander stops at Mutchilba for morning tea. Orders are taken on board in the morning so your <u>smoko</u> will be ready on arrival.

11.00am There's a short stop at the railway station in Dimbulah to have a look at the museum that has been set up in the old station building. Snacks are available.

1.15pm The train arrives in Almaden which is the end of the train trip for Wednesday. Lunch is at the Railway Hotel which is directly across the road from the railway station. If you're staying in Almaden then that's the end of the day for you. Those going to Chillagoe will be transferred by bus after lunch.

3pm If you're staying in Chillagoe and doing the limestone cave and town tour you'll be picked up for your tour.

5.30pm Those on the cave and town tour in Chillagoe will be returned to their local accommodation and can relax for the rest of the day. Dinner and breakfast is included.

Next morning Chillagoe passengers will be returned to Almaden to re-join the Savannahlander.

Thursday: Day 2 Train departs Almaden at 8am for the next <u>leg</u> of the journey west on the way to Mt Surprise and the Undara lava tubes.

Note: Lunch and morning tea are at own expense.

Source: Savannahlander itinerary.
Personal records

Understanding itineraries   Circle a letter or write an answer for questions 1 to 8.

1. What pertinent advice is given to passengers prior to leaving Cairns Central station?
    A   the first passenger stop after Cairns Central is Freshwater station
    B   no food is available at the station or on the train
    C   the train arrives at Stoney Creek Falls at 7:30am
    D   passengers departure times may vary up to 15 minutes

2. After leaving Cairns Station the first new passengers can join the train at
    A   Freshwater station   B   Barron Falls station
    C   Kuranda station   D   Mareeba station

3. What do Savannahlander passengers have the opportunity to do in Almaden?
    A   visit the railway museum   B   take a bus tour of Almaden
    C   have lunch at the local hotel   D   visit limestone caves

4. Train travellers who participated in the Barron River Rover trip should wait at
    A   Cairns Central station   B   Barron Falls station
    C   Kuranda station   D   Mareeba station

5. The Savannahlander stops at Mutchilba for a *smoko*?
    Smoko is a colloquial term for
    A   an opportunity for smokers to leave the train for a cigarette
    B   a break from an activity to have refreshments
    C   a short engine refuelling period
    D   a stage in a journey for an alternate activity

6. A major reason for the short stop at Kuranda station is to let passengers
    A   view the Barron River Falls
    B   buy snacks and refreshments
    C   going on to Mareeba leave the train
    D   enjoy the station gardens

7. How long between the arrival time at Kuranda and the arrival time at Almaden?

    Write your answer on the line. _____

8. As used in the text, which word has a similar meaning to *leg* (last line)?
    A   stage   B   peg   C   instalment   D   passage

Lit Tip 12 – Improve your Literacy skills   Plurals for years and initials

The general rule is that you should **NOT** use an apostrophe to form the plurals of nouns, abbreviations, or dates made up of numbers: just add -s.

Examples: 1990s, in the 80s, CDs, SUVs, MPs
We learn the three Rs at school. In the maths test we all got As.

Highlight the correct form.
There were seven (JPs, JP's, JPS) in the courthouse.
Only four (POW's, POWS, POWs) returned after the war.
The depression of the (1930's, 1930s, 1930S) caused much misery.

Understanding Year 8 Comprehension
A. Horsfield © Five Senses Education © W. Marlin

The Hundred-Foot Journey

India 1940s

. . . the essence of Indian life. Train carriages are split between men and women and commuters literally hang from windows and doors as trains ratchet down the rails. The trains are so crowded there isn't room for commuters' lunch boxes, which arrive in separate trains after rush hour. These tiffin boxes – over two million battered tin cans with lids – smelling of daal and gingery cabbage and black pepper rice and sent on by loyal wives – are sorted, stacked into trundle carts and delivered with the utmost precision to each insurance clerk and bank teller throughout Bombay.

It was on the eve of World War II that my grandfather set up his clapboard house in the slums of Nepean Sea Road. Bombay was the backroom of the Allies' Asian war effort, and soon millions of soldiers from around the world were passing through its gates. For many soldiers it was their last moments of peace before the torrid fighting in Burma and the Philippines, and young men cavorted about Bombay's coastal roads, cigarettes hanging from their lips and ogling the girls who worked in Chowpatty Beach area.

It was my grandmother's idea to sell them snacks, and my grandfather eventually agreed, adding to the tiffin business a string of food stalls on bicycles, obile snack bars that rushed from bathing soldiers at Juhu Beach on Friday evening to the rush-hour crush outside the Churchgate train station. They sold sweets made from nuts and hone, milky tea, but mostly they sold bhelpuri, a newspaper cone of puffed rice, chutney potatoes, onions, tomatoes, mint and coriander, all mixed together and slathered with spices.

Delicious I tell you, and not surprisingly the snack bicycles became a commercial success. And so encouraged by their good fortune my grandparents cleared an abandoned lot on the far side of Nepean Sea Road. It was there they erected a primitive roadside restaurant. They built a kitchen of three tandoori ovens – and a <u>bank</u> of charcoal fires on which rested kadais (bowl-shaped frying pan) of mutton masala – all under a US Army tent. In the shade of a banyan tree they also set up some rough tables and slung hammocks.

Adapted from The Hundred-Foot Journey, an ebook version p. 12 -14

Understanding narratives

Circle a letter to answer questions 1 to 8.

1. The tiffins did not travel with their owners on the train. Why?
   A they weren't prepared prior to the owners' departures
   B the smell of spicy food was not acceptable on passenger trains
   C the trains were so overcrowded there was no room for the tiffins
   D it was beneath the dignity of clerks and tellers to carry their own food

2. The cultural setting of the passage highlights the
   A affluence of the American soldiers
   B degradation most Indians endure
   C inferior quality of food available for workers
   D economic and class divisions in Bombay

3. The narrator's grandparents could best be described as
   A desperate   B entrepreneurial C fraudulent   D rudimentary

4. In which order did events in the passage occur?
   1. American soldiers are stationed in Bombay
   2. a scheme to sell food from bicycles is set up
   3. tiffin boxes are delivered by cart to city workers
   4. the grandparents take over a block of land

   A 3, 1, 2, 4   B 4, 3, 2, 1   C 1, 3, 2, 4   D 3, 2, 1, 4

5. What was the grandmother's innovative idea?
   A to increase the size of the tiffin delivery business
   B to clear an abandoned block of land
   C to erect a primitive roadside restaurant
   D to sell Indian snacks to the soldiers

6. Which word best relates to the mood created in the extract?
   A bustling   B frustration   C contentment   D chaos

7. The word *bank* as used in paragraph 4 refers to
   A a financial institution   B the gradient of the land
   C an array of similar items   D being reliable or dependable

8. The grandparents set up their restaurant *all under a US Army tent* (paragraph 4).
   In the context of the passage what does this suggests about the grandparents?
   A they had cordial relations with the US troops
   B they were not averse to taking advantage of a situation
   C they saw themselves as part of the war effort
   D they were not to be trusted

Lit Tip 13 – Improve your Literacy skills   Mood (or atmosphere)

Did you have a problem with Q 6? In fiction mood refers to the feelings the text creates in the reader's mind. Writers use the setting, descriptions and words to create a certain mood or atmosphere for the reader. In a story or novel mood can change.

Mood can be expressed in such terms as dark, light, rushed, suspenseful and chaotic.

Circle the word that best relates to the mood created in *Coketown* (Passage 2).

   humdrum   repression   hopefulness   calm   gloom   tenacity

In plays and films mood can be created with the help of dialogue, sets, lights and music.

Understanding Year 8 Comprehension
A. Horsfield © Five Senses Education © W. Marlin

What are water bears?

Researchers have successfully revived microscopic creatures that have been kept frozen for 30 years! What were they?

Tardigrades! Tardigrades, also known as water bears or moss piglets, are tiny water-dwelling organisms. They are segmented with eight legs and measure 1 mm in length. They eat by sucking the juices of plants such as mosses, lichens, liverworts and algae.

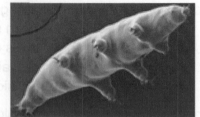

Water bears look like caterpillars with four pairs of legs that have curving claws. Their legs aren't jointed so they amble around in a waddling movement, which is why their scientific name literally means "slow-stepper". Usually they are slightly clearish looking but you can also see food pass through their digestive tract when they feed so they may look green, reddish, brown, or blue-green.

Japanese scientists recently revived the creatures from frozen moss samples collected in Antarctica in 1983. The samples had been stored at minus-20° Celcius for over 30 years.

Two water bears were resuscitated. One of them died after 20 days, but the other went on to successfully reproduce with a third specimen hatched from a frozen egg. It laid 19 eggs of which 14 hatched successfully.

They are known as extremophiles, meaning that they can live in places on Earth that most creatures couldn't handle. They can endure temperatures of absolute zero, pressure higher than that of the deepest oceans, radiation that would kill all other animals, can even live in a vacuum in space for several days and they can go without food or water for more than 10 years!

When they are frozen they enter into a state called <u>cryptobiosis</u>, in which their metabolic processes shut down, and they show no signs of visible life.

Scientists like tardigrades because they are somewhat like jellyfish but easier to study, find, and culture. Water bears have a clearly defined nervous system and digestive system but they lack a circulatory system and respiratory system; so no breathing or pumping blood.

The previous survival record for adult tardigrades under frozen conditions was eight years, and a much earlier study had suggested that the upper limit for survival under normal atmospheric conditions was about 10 years.

There are now plans to work on examining damage to the water bear's genes and its recovery functions to achieve a better understanding of long-term survival mechanisms.

Many bears hibernate for the winter but the smallest '<u>bear</u>' in the world can hibernate for decades before coming back to life!

Adapted from: Daily Telegraph reprinted in Sydney Morning Herald Mon 19/01/16 p 3,
infinitespider.com/tardigrades-introducing-moss-piglet-water-bear/

Understanding explanations

1. What are tardigrades most like?
   - A   caterpillars
   - B   bears
   - C   piglets
   - D   liverworts

2. Tardigrades are known as extremophiles because they
   - A   are small and difficult to locate
   - B   have unusual physical characteristics
   - C   can survive in a very wide range of harsh conditions
   - D   behave in a manner unlike other creatures

3. How long can an active tardigrade go without food or water?
   - A   several days
   - B   20 days
   - C   8 years
   - D   10 years

4. What is cryptobiosis?
   - A   a digestive disease
   - B   a state of suspended animation
   - C   an immune system
   - D   a form of hypothermia

5. In the last sentence 'bear' is in inverted commas.
   What is the reason for this?
   - A   to avoid confusion with any of the tardigrade's alternative names
   - B   to indicate that the tardigrade may not be the smallest bear
   - C   to make readers aware that the tardigrade is not a real bear
   - D   to indicate that the tardigrade may not be the smallest bear

6. According to the text which statement is CORRECT?
   - A   Tardigrades do not need to breathe.
   - B   Once tardigrades show no signs of life they cannot be revived.
   - C   The tardigrade record for surviving in a frozen state is 10 years.
   - D   Most tardigrades are green in colour.

7. Tardigrades do NOT have a
   - A   nervous system
   - B   circulatory system
   - C   digestive system
   - D   reproductive system

8. What is a likely reason scientists are interested in doing research into tardigrades?
   - A   to find ways to prolong the life of tardigrades
   - B   to improve space travel conditions
   - C   to improve living conditions in Antarctica
   - D   to ascertain if tardigrade capabilities have a human application

Lit Tip 14 – Improve your Literacy skills   Morphemes

Morphemes are the smallest units of meaning in English. There are either free morphemes or bound morphemes.

Free morphemes are separate words that cannot be broken down into other meaningful parts such as cat, truck and million.

Bound morphemes cannot stand alone as words such as ex/cept (two morphemes).
Unaided consists of three morphemes: *un*, *aid* and *ed*. Two of these cannot stand alone.
An affix is a bound morpheme which is attached to a free morpheme for meaning.

How many morphemes in this sentence?
The non-perishable goods are being taken from the storeroom. _____

How many syllables? _____

Note: do not confuse syllables with morphemes.

Understanding Year 8 Comprehension
A. Horsfield © Five Senses Education © W. Marlin

The Vanilla Island

Vanilla is an essence and a product of the vanilla orchids, a native to Mexico, from which commercial vanilla flavouring is derived. It is the only orchid widely used for industrial purposes both in the food industry and in the cosmetic industry.

Blooming occurs only when the plants are fully grown. Each flower opens up in the morning and closes late in the afternoon on the same day, never to re-open. The fruit is termed "vanilla bean", but is not related to the common greengrocer's bean. Rather, the vanilla fruit is technically an elongate. It ripens gradually for 8 to 9 months after flowering, eventually turning black in colour and giving off a strong aroma. Each pod contains thousands of minute seeds, and both the pods and seeds within are used to create vanilla flavouring.

Vanilla grows best in a hot, humid climate from sea level to an elevation of 1500 m. The ideal climate has moderate rainfall, 15 - 30 cm, evenly distributed through 10 months of the year. Optimum temperatures for cultivation are 15 - 30°C during the day and 15 - 20°C during the night. Ideal humidity is around 80%. Most successful vanilla growing and processing is done in the region within 10° to 20° of the equator.

The Society Islands are part of French Polynesia, the capital being Papeete on Tahiti.

One of the islands in the Society group is Taha'a. It is known as "The Vanilla Island" and produces 70% to 80% of all of French Polynesia's vanilla which is of very high quality. The island always has a fragrance of vanilla and hibiscus.
The current production of vanilla for all French Polynesia is about 25 tonnes annually, but less than a century ago it was at least six times this amount.

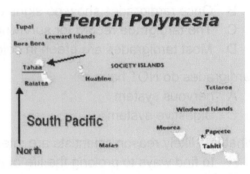

Taha'a and Ra'latea are believed to be the first islands settled in French Polynesia by people most likely from Samoa. They are encircled by the same reef and it is believed that once they were a single island. The vast lagoon is dotted with many islets (*motu*).

Captain Cook first visited these shores in 1769 aboard the Endeavour but returned in 1774 and then again in 1777 en route to Hawaii that proved to be his final voyage.

Vanilla, is now grown commercially in far north Queensland, and is reputed to be of a high quality.

Adapted from: information provided on MSY Wind Spirit, https://en.wikipedia.org/wiki/Vanilla_(genus)
Illustration of Vanilla planifolia by Matilda Smith (1854-1926), from Curtis's Botanical Magazine, Vol. 117.

Understanding reports

Circle a letter or write an answer for questions 1 to 8.

1. The vanilla orchid of Taha'a originated in
   - A Hawaiii
   - B Mexico
   - C Samoa
   - D Tahiti

2. Which word best describes the present day state of the vanilla industry of Taha'a?
   - A contracting
   - B steadfast
   - C developing
   - D erratic

3. How many times did Captain Cook visit the Society Islands?
   - A one
   - B two
   - C three
   - D four

4. In which direction would I travel going from Tahiti to Taha'a?
   - A south west
   - B south east
   - C north west
   - D north east

5. What are the ideal conditions for growing the vanilla orchid?

	Day time Temperature	Humidity	Yearly rainfall	Elevation
A	less than 15°C	around 70%	less than 15 cm	over 1500 m
B	15 - 20°C	around 80%	greater than 30 cm	up to 1500 m
C	greater than 30°C	60% to 80%	15 – 30 cm	1500 m
D	15 - 30°C	about 80%	15 – 30 cm	up to 1500 m

6. According to the text which statement is CORRECT?
   - A The hibiscus flower is important in Taha'a cosmetic industry.
   - B The vanilla orchid pod is often incorrectly referred to as a bean.
   - C Each vanilla pod bears just one seed.
   - D The vanilla orchid stays open for eight or nine days.

7. What is the Polynesian word for a very small island?
   Write your answer on the line. _____

8. What is a brief definition of the term *en route* (paragraph 7)?
   - A voyage of discovery
   - B break in a journey
   - C departing for
   - D on the way

Understanding Year 8 Comprehension
A. Horsfield © Five Senses Education © W. Marlin

Read the report *Space weather.*

Space weather

Since the mid-1960s, interest in observing, understanding, and predicting solar activity has increased. This has given rise to a new field called "Space Weather."

Space weather originates from the Sun. It generally refers to all solar activities such as sunspots and solar flares, and the effects they may have on the Earth. The intensity varies from time to time, sometimes strong and sometimes weak. "Good weather" means a calm period of solar activities, while "bad weather" is a period of frequent and disturbed activities which may affect telecommunications, navigation and power systems on Earth and the operations of satellites or spacecraft.

Solar cycles
Solar activity is periodic. A solar cycle (also called a sunspot cycle) is approximately an 11-year period with increasing and decreasing sunspot numbers. Each cycle starts from the time of minimum activity. The cycle numbering system dates back to the eighteenth century. The current solar cycle is cycle 23.

Sunspots
Sunspots are dark areas on the Sun's surface with relatively low temperatures (compared with other parts of the Sun) and strong magnetic fields. They normally appear in groups. The number of sunspots is usually taken as an indicator of solar activity. It increases significantly and can reach hundreds at the peak of a solar cycle.

Solar flares
A solar flare is a violent solar activity. Its occurrence is related to a sudden burst of electromagnetic waves and a vast amount of charged particles from the Sun. These electromagnetic waves can affect Earth's telecommunications, radio broadcasts and navigation systems. Sometimes, charged particles can also endanger the operations of spacecraft and satellites, and expose astronauts to higher amounts of radiation.

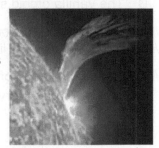

Solar winds
The Sun releases tremendous energy. Solar wind refers to this released energy in the form of charged particles at high speed, reaching several hundred kilometres per second. While the magnetic field on the Earth (which traps charged particles encircling the Earth into radiation belts) normally _____(7)_____ our planet from the solar wind, it may be deformed in the event of violent solar wind, resulting in a geomagnetic storm on Earth.

Geomagnetic storms
A geomagnetic storm occurs when a violent solar wind hits the Earth and severely distorts the Earth's magnetic field. Geomagnetic storms can seriously affect radio broadcasts and navigation systems, and paralyse electric grids on Earth. During the great geomagnetic storm in 1989, electricity was suspended for 9 hours in Quebec and a number of American satellites were taken out of service. The last significant geomagnetic storm occurred in October 2003 when intense solar flares erupted from the Sun, causing a Japanese communications satellite to shut down temporarily.

Adapted from: http://www.hko.gov.hk/education/edu05spacewx/ele_spacewxe.htm

Understanding reports

Circle a letter to answer questions 1 to 8.

1. How long is a solar cycle?

   A 12 months   B 11 years   C 23 years   D 30 years

2. Which feature of space weather has the most effect on human space activities?

   A sunspots   B solar flares
   C solar winds   D geomagnetic storms

3. When was the earliest dating of a solar cycle?

   A 23 years before this text was written   B just prior to 1989
   C eighteenth century   D October 2003

4. Which feature of space weather has the most effect on communications and power supply?

   A sunspots   B solar flares
   C solar winds   D geomagnetic storms

5. What is a feature of solar winds?

   A high speed charged particles emanating from the sun
   B sudden bursts of electromagnetic waves
   C a strengthening of the earth's magnetic field
   D a change in the number and intensity of sunspots

6. A serious outcome of the 2003 geomagnetic storm was

   A an unexpected break in 'good solar' weather
   B a disruption to the earth's magnetic field
   C increased exposure from radiation for astronauts
   D an extended blackout in the Quebec region

7. A word has been deleted from the text.
   Which word would be best suited to the space (7)?

   A deforms   B destroys   C protects   D   paralyses

8. In a period of high solar flare activity which of these services would be most disrupted?

   A television networks   B primary production suppliers
   C power providers   D emergency services

Lit Tip 16 – Improve your Literacy skills   Interjections

An interjection is one of the eight major parts of speech. It is used to convey emotion.

They can be used at the beginning or the end of a sentence followed by an exclamation mark (but not always).

Examples and their applications

Boo – to scare someone	Hmm – thinking or hesitating	bah – showing contempt
Aha – understanding	Oops – accidental outcome	Oh – mild surprise
Cheerio – goodbye	Good grief – disbelief	Grr – anger

Add a suitable interjection for these sentences.

_____! That's my pencil. _____! You're on my toe! _____! Wait there.

Interjections are not normally used in formal writing.

Understanding Year 8 Comprehension
A. Horsfield © Five Senses Education © W. Marlin

Hammerheads

Hammers have two parts - the hammer handle and hammer head. Beyond that are subtleties that only engineers and blacksmiths might appreciate. Every carpenter, every machinist, and every home handy person has at least one hammer in the tool kit. The hammerhead, the heaviest striking surface, is used for most work.

A sledge hammer is a tool with a large, flat, often metal head, attached to a handle. Sledge hammers have two identical faces. The size of its head allows a sledgehammer to apply more force than other hammers of similar size. It has the ability to distribute force over a wide area. This is in contrast to other types of hammers, which concentrate force in a relatively small area. Sledge hammers were used extensively in early railroad building.

A mallet is a hammer with a head that is often made of rubber or wood. Wooden mallets are used in woodwork, cabinet making, securing pieces of wood together and driving chisels into other wooden surfaces. A wooden mallet is also used to strike and shape various tools and metals. This is because it will not damage the surface of the tool or metal as readily as hammers. The wood also acts as a shock absorber and takes much of the impact when striking. Most other hammer types have only one face. The opposite side of the hammerhead is called the peen. The face of a hammer is slightly <u>convex</u> or crowned. Too much crown causes nails to skate across the face when struck. Some framing hammers have a cross-hatched face to reduce slipping and allow heavy blows. Handle sockets or eyes have a slight taper, wider at the top than the bottom.

Peens
Peens come in many styles and are designed for many different purposes. Machinists' hammers have round or ball peens; one use is to expand the head of a solid rivet. The common blacksmith's hammer has a cross-peen (flat blade) used for metal working.

Carpenters' hammers include a claw peen for pulling nails.

Handle
Many hammers still use handles of hickory or ash. Fiberglass handles may be bonded to the hammerhead with strong adhesives or strap fastenings. Steel handles are forged from the same continuous piece of steel as the hammerhead and covered with a cushioning grip.
The older wooden handles are fixed in the eye of the hammerhead with a double wedge. The first wedge - a wooden wedge - follows the long axis and expands the handle to the sides of the eye. The second wedge - of steel - splits the wooden wedge crossways and expands the handle toward the ends of the eye.

Temper
An unseen but essential quality of every hammerhead is <u>temper</u>. Eye walls should be tempered much softer than face or peen. Striking faces must be hard enough to resist denting. Incorrectly tempered hammers can shatter like glass or dent so quickly that they leave scars in the work.

Sources: https://en.wikipedia.org/wiki/Sledgehammer
http://hamww.ehow.com/about_5367760_parts-hammer.html#ixzz2gcfMPc1V

Understanding explanations

Circle a letter to answer questions 1 to 8.

1. Who is most likely to have most use for a mallet?
   A woodworker   B railroad worker C mechanic   D machinist

2. The feature that most often dictates the purpose a hammer will be used for is its
   A handle   B mass   C peen   D structure

3. How does a steel hammer differ from most other hammers?
   A its head is taped to the handle
   B the head and handle are not separate components
   C its use is limited to blacksmith work situations
   D the handle socket is slightly tapered

4. You read: (an) *essential quality of every hammerhead is temper*
   In the context of the passage what does *temper* refer to
   A an innate balance between handle and head
   B the precision in which the hammer is used
   C a tendency for the head to fly off the handle
   D the hardness and elasticity of a metal

5. Who is most likely to have most use for a hammer with a cross-peen?
   A cabinet maker   B carpenter   C mechanic   D blacksmith

6. I have a hammer that has an ash handle and a steel head with a claw peen.
   What is one function of such a hammer?
   A driving a chisel into woodwork   B expanding the head of a rivet
   C removing nails from timber   D driving a wedge into a peen

7. You read: *the face of a hammer is slightly convex* (paragraph 5).
   What is the antonym of *convex*?
   A concuss   B contrast   C convent   D concave

8. According to the text which statement is **NOT** correct?
   A Each particular hammer has just one use.
   B Steel hammers have a special grip to cushion impact.
   C Most hammers concentrate their impact over a small area.
   D The steel hammer does not require an eye.

Lit Tip 17 – Improve your Literacy skills   Nouns and gender

Most English nouns do not have grammatical gender. It is common practice for nouns referring to people not to have separate forms for men and women. Traditionally some nouns had different forms - waiter / waitress. Nowadays it is more acceptable to use a neutral form.

Look at this table.	male form	female form	neutral form
	actor	actress	
	headmaster	headmistress	headteacher (principal)

In the past some jobs were done only by men (fireman) or women (nurse). Neutral words are more 'politically correct'. There is often more than one alternative.

What is the 'correct' term for secretary? _____, heroine? _____,

songstress? _____, cowboy? _____, hostess? _____

It is acceptable to use pronouns and possessives that show gender (he, she, hers, him).

Understanding Year 8 Comprehension
A. Horsfield © Five Senses Education © W. Marlin

Heat Wave

Waves of heat ripple
through spaced-out air
The elderly gasp like landed fish

People stroll in shopping mall cool
while their countless cars
roast on concrete

Chocolate swoons
over parboiled lemons
straight from trees

Like a buckled rail track
a trail of ants wind from
nowhere on its journey for water

Cockroaches breach the kitchen
I answer the door to the frenzied
buzzing of flies

A mirror, always unstable
loses a leg when the glue melts
Shatters

Adds to the gloom
of long-range forecasts
worse than any yet recorded

A stunned bird falls into
the mouth of a <u>languid</u> cat
Straw lawns crunch underfoot

Ground cover rolls
green leaves into grey scrolls
bearing only <u>bad news</u>

Trees bake and burn
in this oven set on high
Fall into an early autumn

Arsonists smudge charcoal over
the land, survey their handiwork
with furtive satisfaction

Coolers roar like landing aircraft
Europe freezes in the coldest
pinch for years

Jennifer Chrystie

Our thanks to Jennifer Chrystie for permission to include her poem in this publication.
From: Weight of Snow by Jennifer Chrystie 2013

Understanding poetry

Circle a letter to answer questions 1 to 8.

1. The poem mostly creates pictures of
   - A depressive conditions
   - B parched landscapes
   - C climatic extremes
   - D torrid weather

2. Which of these lines from the poem is **NOT** an example of a simile?
   - A The elderly gasp like landed fish
   - B *cars / roast on concrete*
   - C *Coolers roar like landing aircraft*
   - D Like a buckled rail track / a trail of ants wind from / nowhere

3. A languid cat (stanza 8) is one that has
   - A no inclination to pursue activity
   - B displayed feelings of respect
   - C an awareness of wrong doing
   - D an expectation of being forgiven

4. In stanza 9 the poet refers to <u>bad news</u>. What is the bad news?
   - A autumn has not yet arrived
   - B bushfires devastate the landscape
   - C the heat wave is unrelenting
   - D an infestation of cockroaches

5. What does the poet contrast with the people in shopping malls?
   - A cars parked without protection
   - B the weather in Europe
   - C the frenzied buzzing of flies
   - D trees bake and burn

6. What is suggested by the poet's tone when she says (stanza 7):
   Adds to the gloom/ of long-range forecasts/ worse than any yet recorded?
   - A open disbelief
   - B indifference to her plight
   - C mild indignation
   - D reluctant acceptance

7. The poet considers the idea that *Europe freezes* while she endures a *heat wave* as
   - A pertinent
   - B bizarre
   - C predictable
   - D justified

8. The exploits of the arsonist (stanza 11) are
   - A clandestine
   - B prophetic
   - C intrepid
   - D blatant

Lit Tip 18 – Improve your Literacy skills   The prefix *para*

The prefix para has several usual meanings.

Para may refer to something 'beyond or resembling' but similar to the usual meaning of the base word.

Examples: paranormal – beyond normal experience
                 parable – a meaning beyond the literal narrative

It also carries the meaning of protecting. **Examples:** parasol, parachute

It may suggest by the side of or nearby. **Examples:** paragraph, parallel, paramedic

Find the meaning of:

paradox _____

paraglider _____

Understanding Year 8 Comprehension
A. Horsfield © Five Senses Education © W. Marlin

Deposit on drink containers

Everyone has seen discarded drink containers along roadsides.

More than 82% of the community supports a national container deposit scheme. Show our ministers what you think about a Container Deposit Scheme. Send your concerns to your local member.

Did you know, bottles and cans are a significantly smaller proportion of litter in South Australia than NSW or Victoria? Conservationists say this is evidence the state's 10c refund for recyclable containers works.

The new data comes as a meeting of state and federal environment ministers consider the effects of introducing a national container deposit system similar to South Australia's scheme.

The state litter breakdown is drawn from data collected by Clean Up Australia of litter removed at 752 sites on the 2012 Clean Up Australia Day, which has been analysed by CSIRO researchers.

They found bottles and cans accounted for one in every 12 pieces of rubbish collected in South Australia. In NSW bottles and cans were about one in every three pieces of litter and in Victoria about one in five.

CSIRO researchers said South Australia had a significantly lower component of beverage containers in the Clean Up data than any other state. "If you pick up an item of litter in NSW it is four times more likely to be a beverage container than in South Australia which has a container deposit scheme," they said.

Jeff Angel from the Total Environment Centre, who has long campaigned for a national container deposit system, said, "These findings show clearly that the container deposit system in South Australia is making an impact. No alternative suggested by industry can solve this problem."

The Northern Territory recently lost a court battle to protect its deposit scheme after it was challenged by major drink companies. The beverage industry says a national 10c refund would be costly and raise drink prices for consumers.

The council of environment ministers recently agreed to develop an "impact statement" on the implications of a national container deposit scheme. The Federal Environment Minister said he'd look seriously at any proposal to discourage litter, but it would work only if there was an agreement with the states.

(_____ (6) _____)

Idea from: http://www.smh.com.au/environment/litter-data-recycles-case-for-bottle-and-can-refund-20130410-2hlty.html
http://www.cleanup.org.au/au/Whatelsewesupport/why-do-we-need-a-container-deposit-legislation-.html

Understanding expositions

Circle a letter or write an answer for questions 1 to 8.

1. Per population size, which state or territory has the least drink container roadside litter?

   A VIC   B NT   C NSW   D SA

2. Everyone has seen discarded drink containers (line 1)
   (Tick a box.)

   This sentence is an example of HIGH ☐ or LOW ☐ modality. (Check out **Lit Tip 19**.)

3. Paragraph 6 begins with the word *They.*
   They is a pronoun which refers to

   A conservationists   B federal environment ministers
   C Clean Up Australia volunteers   D anyone who discards a drink container

4. Which argument is presented for not having a deposit on drink containers?

   A ten cents (10c) is not enough to encourage people to return used containers
   B a refund scheme will add extra costs for the consumer
   C suppliers will have to have an ample supply of cash to pay for the refund
   D it's too much effort and inconvenience to return used drink containers

5. The writer provides a variety of statistical data.
   The most likely reason for this is to

   A give credibility to his opinion
   B bamboozle the reader with irrelevant facts
   C create feelings of scepticism to any proposal
   D employ a subterfuge to achieve his intended result

6. The final sentence (6) has been deleted from the text.
   Which sentence would be a suitable conclusion to the text?

   A Pick up some roadside litter today.
   B NSW should adopt the Container Deposit Scheme.
   C Support the call for a Container Deposit Scheme.
   D If the drink's in a tin put the tin in a bin!

7. Which word in the text is an all inclusive word for soft drinks, water, milk, tea and coffee?
   Write your answer on the line. _____

8. How does the writer feel about the idea of having a deposit on drink containers?

   A he is strongly in favour of the idea
   B he thinks it could be a reasonable idea
   C he has reservations about the effectiveness of such a scheme
   D he regards the scheme as an infringement of personal liberties

---

Lit Tip 19 – Improve your Literacy skills   Modal verbs

You need to understand how to use modality effectively, especially when writing persuasive text, such as discussions, expositions and advertisements and responsive texts such as reviews. Modal verbs give the reader (or listener) information about the degree of conviction or certainty involved.

Low modal verbs show less certainty: I might leave early.

High modal verbs show a high degree of certainty: I will leave early.

Use **L** or **H** to indicate the modality of these sentences.

You could try again. ( )	I will do it myself. ( )	He always sings at home. ( )
Bill has to feed the cat. ( )	We could read a book. ( )	She may need help. ( )

Understanding Year 8 Comprehension
A. Horsfield © Five Senses Education © W. Marlin

The green thing

Checking out at the store, the young cashier suggested to the older woman that she should bring her own shopping bags because plastic bags weren't good for the environment.

The woman apologised and explained, "We didn't have this green thing back in my earlier days."

The cashier responded, "That's our problem today. <u>Your generation did not care enough to save our environment for future generations</u>."

She was right - our generation didn't have the green thing in its day. Back then, we returned milk bottles, soft drink bottles to the store. The store sent them back to the plant to be washed and sterilised and refilled, so it could use the same bottles over and over. So they really were recycled. We refilled writing pens with ink instead of buying a new pen, and we replaced the razor blades in a razor instead of throwing away the whole razor just because the blade got <u>dull</u>. But we didn't have the green thing back in our day.

We walked up stairs, because we didn't have an escalator in every shop and office building. We walked to the grocery store and didn't climb into a car every time we had to go two blocks. But she was right. We didn't have the green thing in our day.

Back then, we washed the baby's nappies because we didn't have the throw-away kind. We dried clothes on a line, not in an energy gobbling machine - wind and solar power really did dry our clothes back in our early days. Kids got hand-me-down clothes from their brothers or sisters, not always brand-new clothing.

Back then, <u>we had one TV, or radio, in the house - not a TV in every room</u>. The TV had a small screen the size of a handkerchief not a screen the size of a wall.

In the kitchen, we blended and stirred by hand because we didn't have electric machines to do everything for us. When we packaged a fragile item to send in the post, we used wadded up old newspapers to cushion it, not Styrofoam or plastic bubble wrap. Back then, we didn't fire up an engine and burn petrol just to cut the lawn. We used a push mower that ran on human power. We exercised by working so we didn't need to go to a gym to run on treadmills that operate on electricity.

We drank water from a tap when we were thirsty instead of demanding a plastic bottle flown in from another country. We accepted that a lot of food was seasonal and didn't expect it to be flown in from thousands of air kilometres. We actually cooked food that didn't come out of a packet, tin or plastic wrap and we would even wash our own vegetables and chop our own salad.

Back then, people took the tram or a bus, and kids rode their bikes to school or walked instead of turning their mothers into a 24-hour taxi service. But isn't it sad the current generation laments how wasteful we old folks were just because we didn't have the green thing back then?

Source unknown

Understanding discussions

Circle a letter to answer questions 1 to 8.

1. The young cashier's comments to the older woman could be considered
   A to be displaying an understanding of environmental issues
   B considerate by informing the older woman the error of her ways
   C to be totally inappropriate in the circumstance
   D relevant considering the older woman's ignorance

2. The older woman states *we had one TV, or radio, in the house -- not a TV in every room.* By making this point she is
   A disparaging of the excesses of consumerism
   B thrilled by the scope of opportunities now available
   C being envious of modern opportunities
   D feeling threatened by developments in electronic homewares

3. The writer states: *the blade got <u>dull</u>* (paragraph 4).
   In this context what does *dull* mean?
   A lacking shine   B no longer sharp
   C slow moving   D indistinctly felt

4. The older woman's tone when she repeats *we didn't have the green thing back in our day* is one of
   A vague bewilderment   B smug superiority
   C righteous annoyance   D mild sarcasm

5. Who is the target of much of the older woman's criticism?
   A the young cashier   B elderly people of her vintage
   C the modern generation   D supermarket operators

6. The older woman's reaction to the comment *Your generation did not care enough to save our environment for future generations* could best be described as one of
   A a rationalisation of her present situation B regret at her inconsiderate behaviour
   C guilt arising from her inaction   D a justification for changing her ways

7. The older woman would most likely see the changes that have occurred as
   A exciting   B wasteful   C beneficial   D irrelevant

8. What is the writer implying about modern society?
   A its young people are reluctant to speak out on environmental issues
   B it has been burdened by the mistakes of another generation
   C there is little appreciation of the soundness of many earlier practices
   D its ways are superior to previous ways of understanding the environment

---

Lit Tip 20 – Improve your Literacy skills   **Writing the time**

The definers of time (am, pm) are seen in a wide variety of forms. For example: A.M. and a.m.

Some educational institutions recommend no space between the am/pm definer and do not use full stops in either term : 8am, 7pm. Others may encourage spaces: 5 pm, 2.30 pm.
A full stop, rather than a colon (:), is used between the hours and minutes :11.45pm

To show a time span separate the times with a space, dash, space: 6.30 – 7.00 am or if the time is over noon (12.00) it will be written as 11am – 3pm.

The best advice is to be consistent in your writing.

Understanding Year 8 Comprehension
A. Horsfield © Five Senses Education © W. Marlin

21 Look at these series of *Evolution graphics.*

Evolution

Definitions
Evolution 1: (noun) the process by which different kinds of living organisms are believed
to have developed from earlier forms during the history of the earth
Evolution 2: (noun) the gradual development of something

Understanding graphics

Circle a letter to answer questions 1 to 8.

1. The Graphics **1**, **2** and **4** suggests that human life is
   A   continuing to make beneficial advances
   B   in a continual state of flux
   C   no longer showing signs of development
   D   going from strength to strength

2. Look at this evolutionary graphic.
   What comment is it making on society?

   A   humankind is heading for a calamity
   B   society needs to reassess its options
   C   the quality of life is becoming more enjoyable
   D   hunting is still a critical part of human existence

3. Which is the antonym of *evolution*?
   A   revolution   B   modify   C   transform   D   devolution

4. A suitable caption for graphic **3** would be
   A   The coming of age   B   Wheels of life
   C   Increasing speed   D   A long life

5. Which graphic most clearly focusses on a *gradual development of something* (definition 2)?
   A   Graphic **1**   B   Graphic **2**   C   Graphic **3**   D   Graphic **5**

6. Graphic **4** is most likely depicting
   A   changes in work patterns   B   increasing laziness
   C   the importance of businessmen   D   the under valuing of menial tasks

7. Graphic 6 is most likely depicting the evolution of
   A   hunting   B   writing   C   farming   D   graffiti

8. These four graphics can show the evolution of lighting.
   Use the numbers to show the logical order of the evolution?

   A   1, 2, 4, 3   B   2, 4, 1, 3
   C   **2, 1, 4, 3**   D   2, 1, 3, 4

   1   **2**   **3**   **4**

Understanding Year 8 Comprehension
A. Horsfield © Five Senses Education © W. Marlin

Making a Storyboard?

A storyboard is a written or graphical representation of all of the elements that will be included in a digital story. The storyboard is usually created before work on creating the digital story begins and a written description and graphical depiction of the elements of the story, such as images, text, narration, music and transitions, are added to the storyboard. The elements of the story are arranged in the ____(7)____order in which they will appear. This allows the developer to organise and re-arrange the content for maximum effect.

Creating storyboards is an often overlooked component of digital storytelling and for many beginners, storyboarding may seem like a tedious extra step. However, storyboarding can be a valuable component in the creative process by allowing the developer to organise images and text in a blueprint fashion before the development begins. It allows the user to visualise how the project will be put together and helps to illustrate what holes exist since they can see the entire laid-out plan. Storyboarding also inspires new ideas as well as letting the developer rearrange existing resources before the final development begins and changes are harder to make.

The important thing about storyboards is that they give you a way to decide how you will split up your script into individual pieces so that you can then get a clearer overview of your digital story plan.

Storyboards may be created in a variety of ways, both digitally and manually on paper or artists' boards. Don't worry about how sophisticated (or unsophisticated) it looks nobody but you will see it!

Tips for Success
1. Make sure your storyboard progression is logical and coherent. Even if your video is a "who-done-it?" your audience expects a logical progression to a conclusion. Although plot-twists are exciting, stories that draw conclusions from nothing are unsatisfying.
2. Using an attention-grabber at the beginning of your story can set the tone and get your audience interested. An attention-grabber can be:
    • a question
    • a scenario
    • a tantalising image
3. When creating a storyboard, the visual parts of the frames should be kept simple and the image in each frame should be one that best describes the action taking place. The images can be simple sketches, or images found on the web.

Source: http://digitalstorytelling.coe.uh.edu/page.cfm?id=23&cid=23&sublinkid=37

Understanding procedures   Circle a letter or write an answer for questions 1 to 8.

1. What is a storyboard?
   - A   a graphical representation of sequential elements of a digital story
   - B   a practical method to get those new to storyboarding involved
   - C   a training strategy for those starting off in digital story production
   - D   an unsophisticated comic format for children learning to read

2. What should be an early step in developing digital story?
   - A   deciding on the music
   - B   writing and narrating the text
   - C   drawing the storyboard
   - D   establishing a satisfying conclusion

3. In **Tips for Success** the writer refers to a "*who done it*"?
   In this context to what is he referring?
   - A   the storyboard artist
   - B   an unsatisfactory ending
   - C   an unknown writer
   - D   a fictional crime thriller

4. According to the text which method is **NOT** involved in the creation of a storyboard?
   - A   the incorporation of images from the web
   - B   images devised on artists' boards
   - C   images created manually with pen and paper
   - D   through video camera images

5. In **Tips for Success** one option is to have a *scenario*?
   In this context what is meant by a *scenario*?
   - A   the setting of the story
   - B   a sequential plan
   - C   graphics with an impact
   - D   a possible storyline

6. According to the text the benefit of a storyboard is that it
   - A   conceals any irregularities that may weaken the plot
   - B   allows the user to visualise how the project will be put together
   - C   removes much of the tedious work of digital storytelling
   - D   prevents a waste of time arising from constructive suggestions

7. A word has been deleted from the text.
   Which word would be best suited to the space (7)?
   - A   random
   - B   chronological
   - C   action
   - D   consequential

8. Each frame in a storyboard should
   - A   be visually attractive
   - B   pose questions for the viewer
   - C   simply portray the action taking place
   - D   be detailed and creative

Lit Tip 22 – Improve your Literacy skills   **Hyphens (-)**

The most common use of hyphens is to indicate that two or more words are acting as a single concept to describe the following noun: full-time student, four-wheel-drive vehicle.

Hyphens can also prevent misunderstandings.
Can you see the subtle difference between *three-monthly tests* and *three monthly-tests*?
Try these: *a heavy-metal detector* and a *heavy metal-detector*?

Where would be the most logical place for the hyphen in this term? man eating shark

There is a convention to use hyphens to connect many common terms: two-fifteen, north-west, non-fiction, student-teacher. You should be familiar with these instances.

Understanding Year 8 Comprehension
A. Horsfield © Five Senses Education © W. Marlin

Cannibals' Gold

The wind was freshening as John trudged along a track crowded with miners, experienced as well as new chums, together with scores of Chinese wearing huge brimmed hats, their worldly possessions balanced on long poles.

The dust from hundreds of pairs of feet blew to the side, to settle in a grey cloud on the vegetation alongside the track. From time to time John passed other men returning from the diggings looking exhausted and he was surprised at the number of old white-haired men, many of whom had boots coming apart at the seams. Large numbers of the Chinese were even bare-footed.

Soon John noticed the smoke from dozens of campfires as men boiled their billies and prepared their evening meal. <u>Selecting a likely spot</u> near a group of miners who were obviously returning from the goldfields, he set up his camp and it was not long before he too had made his tea and prepared an evening meal.

Men of all kinds and description continued to file past, heading inland towards the fields, interspersed with packhorses and teams of bullocks and horses drawing wagons and drays, all piled high with stores and provisions.

<u>As the sun dipped</u> low in the western sky, it was accompanied by a sharp drop in the temperature and the wind that had gusted constantly all day and which had taken the heat out of the August sun, suddenly died away. Clouds of brightly coloured rainbow lorikeets flashed noisily above, heading towards their evening roosts. A small flock of pink and grey galahs, a parrot found almost everywhere in the Australian outback, alighted in a tree overhead, squawking loudly as though in protest at the newcomers.

Having filled his pipe, John lit the tobacco and, leaning back on his swag against a nearby tree, idly watched a heavily-laden horse-drawn wagon rumbling and creaking over the rocks and ruts, enveloped in a heavy cloud of dust. As John sipped his tea between puffs of his pipe, one of the men sitting around the fire nearby stood up and wandered over slowly, dusting his hands as he did so.

'G'day mate, 'ow ya goin'?' grinned the friendly newcomer, obviously a miner.

'Very well thanks,' replied John as he glanced over in the man's direction. 'And how is it with you?' He gestured graciously towards a spare patch of ground near the fire.

Ta, mate,' acknowledged the miner, pushing his battered felt hat back off his forehead. 'I was wondering if you could spare a little t'bacca? We're a mite short of the necessaries y'unnerstand. We've been on the road back from the Palmer fer a few days now, but I figure we'll be right once we hit Cooktown <u>termorrer</u>.'

Richard Tomkies

Adapted from: http://www.zeus-publications.com/cannibals_gold.htm
Our thanks to Richard Tomkies for giving permission to use this extract from Cannibals' Gold, 5th Edition, Zeus Publications 2010. Richard recently released True Stories of Early Australia.

Understanding narratives

Circle a letter to answer questions 1 to 8.

1. The attitude of the miners John met at the camp site was one of
   A   cautious acceptance
   B   open hostility
   C   reluctant approval
   D   guarded suspicion

2. The people travelling in the opposite direction along the track to John were mostly
   A   miners who had made their fortune
   B   prospectors who had given up hope of striking it rich
   C   Chinese who had been forced off the diggings
   D   people heading to Palmer to replenish supplies

3. In paragraph 3 you read of John *selecting a likely spot.*
   What would John have most likely have considered in *selecting his likely spot*?
   A   his safety on the isolated goldfields
   B   a location away from the dust created by the goldfields traffic
   C   the pleasure of having the company of fellow miners
   D   gathering inside information on gold prospecting sites

4. What is the main focus of paragraph 5 (*As the sun dipped . . .*)?
   A   it provides a description of bush conditions near the diggings
   B   it hints at the distrust between miners and newcomers
   C   it provides a historical background to a gold rush
   D   it recounts a sequence of events leading up to the evening meal

5. The miners say: *we hit Cooktown termorrer.* (last paragraph)
   The word *termorrer* is an example of
   A   an idiomatic expression
   B   a colloquialism
   C   the vernacular of a non-English speaker
   D   specialised jargon

6. In which order did these events in the extract occur?
   1. John makes himself a cup of tea   2. John notices smoke from a campfire
   3. John lights his pipe for a smoke   4. John invites a miner to sit by his fire

   A   3, 2, 1, 4   B   1, 3, 2, 4   C   2, 1, 3, 4   D   2, 3, 1, 4

7. How was John feeling after his day travelling to the goldfields?
   A   apprehensive   B   intimidated   C   composed   D   circumspect

8. A suitable title for this extract would be
   A   Chinese gold prospectors
   B   The dusty track
   C   Campsite meals
   D   The fortune hunters

Lit Tip 23 – Improve your Literacy skills   *And* after a comma

We often hear that *and* cannot follow a comma, however *and* can be used to join two independent clauses. In the following example the clauses are in brackets.

   (Pippa took driving lessons for six months), and (today she now drives herself to work).

In the next example no comma is required after and because just one independent clause is involved.

   (Pippa took driving lessons for six months) and now drives to work. There are two verbs (took, drives) but only one subject (Pippa).

Bracket the two independent clauses in this sentence.

The storm last night caused lines to come down, and many people were left without power.

Understanding Year 8 Comprehension
A. Horsfield © Five Senses Education © W. Marlin

Spencer Williams

Jazz is a music genre that originated from African American communities of New Orleans in the United States during the late 19th and early 20th centuries. Improvisation is a key aspect of jazz. Basically, improvisation is composing on the spot, in which a singer or instrumentalist invents and freely explores solo melodies over the top of a chord progression played by rhythm section instruments (piano, double bass, drum kit, etc.).

Spencer Williams, (1889 –1965) was one of the earliest black composers to shape jazz as popular music. Many of his songs including "Royal Garden Blues," "Everybody Loves My Baby" and "I Ain't Got Nobody" became anthems of the Jazz Age and the Swing Era - and remain <u>standards</u> today.

Spencer Williams was born in 1889 in New Orleans and educated at St. Charles University. Williams worked in Chicago as a vocalist and pianist as early as 1907. There, he often performed with another pianist, composer, and bandleader: Clarence Williams - no relation. About the time of WWI, Spencer Williams began writing pop songs, such as "Squeeze Me," which he co-composed with Fats Waller.

In 1925 Spencer Williams travelled to Paris and wrote songs for the enticing and attractive American expatriate, Josephine Baker, a star of the famed Follies Bergére. In 1930 Spencer made several recordings, singing and playing the piano with the highly regarded blues guitarists Teddy Bunn and Lonnie Johnson. In 1932 he vacationed in France with his friend Fats Waller. When Waller returned to the US, Williams moved to England, where he remained in residence until 1951, after which he made Sweden his home.

"Basin Street Blues," Williams' 1928 song, celebrates the centre of New Orleans's nightlife, which took its name from the "basin" formed in the back of town from the excavation of building materials by the city's early inhabitants. Later it became his signature song.

"Basin Street Blues"
1946 recording

Basin Street Blues (Words and Music by Spencer Williams 1928)
Won't you come along with me,
To the Mississippi,
We'll take a boat to the land of dreams,
Steam down the river to New Orleans.
The band's there to greet us,
Old friends there to meet us.
Where the rich and the poor folks meet,
Let me take you down to Basin Street.

Basin Street, c.1909. Image in public domain.

Source: http://riverwalkjazz.stanford.edu/program/tishomingo-blues-spencer-williams

Understanding biographies

Circle a letter or write an answer for questions 1 to 8.

1. What is the distinguishing feature of jazz?
   A chord progressions played by rhythm section instruments
   B the way it celebrates New Orleans's nightlife
   C adherents of jazz are virtuosos of many instruments
   D the ability of musicians to create and perform spontaneously

2. Some of Spencer Williams's songs remain standards today. (Paragraph 2)
   As used in the text *standards* are songs that
   A have been written to a prescribed format
   B have remained popular for many decades
   C are the measure by which other songs are judged
   D provide a level of excellence other composers aspire to

3. Williams's final choice of a place to call home was in
   A Sweden   B New Orleans
   C Paris, France   D England

4. Which song became Spencer Williams's signature song?
   A Royal Garden Blues   B Basin Street Blues
   C Everybody Loves My Baby   D I Ain't Got Nobody

5. Basin Street in New Orleans got its name
   A following the success of Williams's song Basin Street Blues
   B symbolising the night life of 1920s New Orleans
   C from an excavation created by local residents for building materials
   D to reflect the shape of sound recordings of the jazz era

6. Write the numbers 1 to 4 in the lines to show the chronological order in which events occurred in the text.
   ____ Williams wrote songs for Josephine Baker, a Follies Bergére star
   ____ Williams becomes a long term resident of England
   ____ Williams attends St. Charles University
   ____ Williams made his home in Sweden

7. During his career Williams was mainly a
   A band leader   B guitarist   C drummer   D pianist

8. Williams co-composed *Squeeze Me* with
   A Fats Waller   B Teddy Bunn
   C Clarence Williams   D Josephine Baker

Lit Tip 24 – Improve your Literacy skills   **Small words from big words**

Many of our common words have their origin in longer words: plane/aeroplane

Car has a longer history including railroad car and carriage.

A submarine can be a sub or a U-boat (undersea boat).

More examples: bus/omnibus, taxi (or cab) /taxicab, fridge/refrigerator

What is the origin of these?   pram _____ , paper _____ ,

tug_____ , van_____ , exam_____ , app_____

Understanding Year 8 Comprehension
A. Horsfield © Five Senses Education © W. Marlin

Spider-man Comic covers

When Spider-Man first appeared in the early 1960s, teenagers in superhero comic books were usually relegated to the role of sidekick to the <u>protagonist</u>. The Spider-Man series broke ground by featuring Peter Parker, the high school student behind Spider-Man's secret identity and with whose "self-obsessions with rejection, inadequacy, and loneliness" young readers could relate. While Spider-Man had all the makings of a sidekick, unlike previous teen heroes such as Bucky (Capt. America) and Robin (Batman), Spider-Man had no superhero mentor like Captain America and Batman. He had to learn for himself that "with great power there must also come great responsibility" - a line included in a text box in the final panel of the first Spider-Man story but later <u>retroactively attributed</u> to his guardian, the late Uncle Ben.

1

2

3

4

Sources: en.wikipedia.org/wiki/Spider-Man

Understanding comic covers   Circle a letter or write an answer for questions 1 to 8.

1. How does Spider-man differ from Batman and Captain America?
    A   he has an outfit that more obviously reflects his identity
    B   he is a teen hero and does not team up with younger assistants
    C   he wad relegated to the role of sidekick in many clashes
    D   he has very low confidence in his worth or ability

2. The covers of the Spider-man comics suggest
    A   horror and brutality   B   realism and plausibility
    C   action and conflict   D   humour and adventure

3. When did Spider-man first appear? _____

4. Spider-man's popularity with comic readers is ascribed to
    A   Spider-man's superhuman powers
    B   their ability to identify with his teenage feelings
    C   the incredible action that takes place in the graphics
    D   the way right triumphs over macabre evil

5. The most likely purpose of the *What if...* question on comics 1 and 2 is to
    A   act as a rhetorical question   B   indicate a foregone conclusion
    C   explore an impossible situation   D   make the reader curious

6. As used in the introductory text what does the term *retroactively attributed* mean?
    A   the saying is credited to a situation prior to events in the first Spider-man edition
    B   there was an element of radioactivity in Spider-man's acquiring of powers
    C   the setting for Spider-man's adventures are in an earlier period
    D   Spider-man's present battles have their genesis in previous conflicts with evil

7. What is a synonym for *protagonist* as used in the introductory paragraph?
    A   victim   B   villain   C   crusader   D   hero

8. The graphics or portrayal of the villains on the comic covers suggest that they are
    A   invincible   B   vengeful   C   malevolent   D   demented

Understanding Year 8 Comprehension
A. Horsfield © Five Senses Education © W. Marlin

Cobbold Gorge

The Cobbold Gorge is located within a 1300 square kilometres cattle station but the gorge is within a 4720 hectare nature reserve where cattle are not permitted to graze. The gorge itself occupies a small area of the reserve. It was discovered by a stockman in 1992.

The gorge is about 6km long, with 30m cliffs on either side, and is two metres wide at its narrowest point. The water maintains a fairly constant level and is fed by springs that seep through the 200 million-year old sandstone and reaches the gorge 30 years later.

Cobbold Gorge was created by a series of geological processes. Sand and mud sediment was deposited on what was then the ocean floor until eventually layers built up to be more than 10 kilometres thick. Movement in the Earth's crust caused the sediments to compress, forming what is called the Hampstead Sandstone. Further movement caused the sedimentary rock to rise and fracture. Torrential, wet season rains over many years spilled torrents of water through the narrow fractures, creating deep gorges and permanent springs and seepages.

The water from Cobbold Creek and its tributaries is funnelled through the very narrow slit in the sandstone known as Cobbold Creek Gorge. The silt laden swirling water forms eddies and whirlpools that wear down the rounded surfaces of the gorge. It is a memorable experience to quietly float beneath the magnificent polished gorge walls, gouged, potholed and carved by the water that gushes through this narrow chasm during the wet season.

Monsoonal rains create turbulent water flows that often carry rocks and debris which can crack the silicon coating allowing swirling, gritty sediment to gouge out new bowl-shaped holes in the softer sandstone. As waters subside a protective silicon glaze develops on the <u>exposed</u> cavity.

As the waters slowly subside they leave behind deposits of silicon, like a coating of dark glass which give the rock a protective layer. In some parts it is over a centimetre thick.

Cobbold Gorge is a very young gorge geologically. Minor movement in recent times (estimated to be 10,000 years ago rather than millions!) have contributed to the formation of the <u>lower reaches of Cobbold Gorge</u> as it is today. Its narrowness indicates that Cobbold Gorge is a young gorge. In fact, it is the youngest known gorge in Queensland.

Sources: http://www.qld.gsa.org.au/rockland.htm, http://www.qld.gsa.org.au/rockland_files/cobbold.pdf
http://www.caravanworld.com.au/destinations/qld/1011/travel-cobbold-gorge-qld, personal experience

1. To a geologist what is the most interesting feature of the Cobbold Gorge?
    A   the silicon glaze on the sandstone
    B   the relatively short existence of the gorge
    C   its discovery late last century
    D   damage done to the walls by monsoonal rains

2. The size of the gorge area nature reserve is
    A   1300 square kilometres   B   4720 hectares
    C   1300 hectares   D   6 kilometres by 30 metres

3. How long does it take the spring water of the gorge to seep through the sandstone?
    A   one wet season   B   3 years
    C   countless decades   D   30 years

4. The apparent age of the Cobbold Gorge is indicated by
    A   its recent discovery by a stockman   B   its water source and water depth
    C   the narrowness of the gorge itself   D   the overall length of the gorge

5. Which is the correct sequence of events that led to the formation of the Cobbold Gorge?
    1. the rock layer fractures and splits creating a water course
    2. movements in the Earth's crust lift the compressed stone
    3. sediment is compressed to form Hampstead Sandstone
    4. sediment forms on the ocean floor

    A   **4, 3, 2, 1**   B   **4, 2, 3, 1**   C   **3, 1, 2, 4**   D   **3, 4, 2, 1**

6. In the last paragraph you read: *the lower reaches of Cobbold Gorge.*
    As used in the text what does *reach* refer to?
    A   making informal contact   B   the touchable distance between walls
    C   the distance of outstretched arms D   a straight stretch of a river

7. Which is an antonym for *exposed* as used in paragraph 5?
    A   protected   B   vulnerable   C   imposed   D   positioned

8. What event initiates the development of new bowl-shaped holes in the gorge walls?
    A   eddies and whirlpools in swirling waters
    B   uplifts and movements in the Earth's crust
    C   objects in turbulent torrents smashing into the gorge walls
    D   the amount and intensity of monsoonal rains

Lit Tip 26 – Improve your Literacy skills   **Spoonerisms**

A **spoonerism** is a verbal error in which a speaker accidently transposes the initial sounds of two or more letters often with a humorous effect (unintentionally).

Examples: you have hissed the mystery lecture/ you have missed the history lecture
can I sew you to another sheet? / can I show you to another seat?

Spoonerisms are named after Reverend Spooner (1844–1930), a college dean, who is reputed to have made these verbal slips quite frequently.

Can you translate these? a lack of pies; flock of bats; know your blows

Understanding Year 8 Comprehension
A. Horsfield © Five Senses Education © W. Marlin

Burial Styles

New Orleans is built on wet flood plains by the Mississippi River. As a result, burials are in tombs above ground level.

Walking through the gate of Lafayette Cemetery in New Orleans (USA) is like walking through a <u>portal</u> into the past. Row upon row of raised tombs, many over a century old, arranged somewhat like houses in a city. The expression "cities of the dead" is used to describe them. As to the large number of names on a tomb, a technique called "<u>unlimited interment</u>" is employed. This is not an uncommon practice around the world.

Once a coffin or casket is placed into a tomb it is sealed with brick and mortar or covered with soil. In the case of family vaults and family tombs, this is merely the process of laying a simple brick "wall" before the vault entrance. The tropical heat in New Orleans turns the sealed tomb into an oven, baking dry all that is inside. Soon the contents turn to ash and cinders.

After the minimum period has gone by, (usually "one year and one day", based upon Judeo-Christian mourning rituals), the space may be re-used, if needed, by simply removing the seal, separating what is left of the human remains and the casket, and pushing the remains to the rear of the vault, or leaving it as debris on the tomb floor.

The casket has been simply disposed of. For that reason this burial style doesn't usually require the use of expensive caskets. Of course, this doesn't take place in the presence of the family who are attending the funeral while this phase of the procedure is performed, and it is always performed in a respectful manner.

Interments are not opened unless they are needed, which may be many years later. However, previous remains are ultimately allowed to simply deteriorate in the bottom of the tomb. Ensuring that remains are left at the burial site, allowing the natural process to take place fulfills the requirements of "ashes to ashes, dust to dust". This process may take decades, although one year is nominal, due to the history of epidemics in the city during the nineteenth century, plus one day out of deference to the family, considered enough time for a body to decompose enough to be handled and fulfill the minimum <u>deference</u> requirements. Remains from all interment material remain at the interment site, unless families request that remains be transferred or handled in a specific manner.

One unusual fact about the cemetery is that many of the names are German, which is interesting because New Orleans was once a French settlement and there was centuries-long rivalry between the French and the Germans. This is simply a sign of the cultural "<u>melting pot</u>" that is New Orleans. As more and more immigrant groups arrived they were invariably subjected to the traditions of earlier cultures, adopting many of the established practices as their own within a few generations.

Source: http://www.lafayettecemetery.org/burial-styles-traditions, private visit

Understanding explanations   Circle a letter or write an answer for questions 1 to 8.

1. An important reason people in New Orleans are **not** buried in graves is because
   - A   the French tradition has a preference for tombs
   - B   cheap caskets can be used instead of expensive ones
   - C   it is more convenient to reuse a tomb than a grave
   - D   the ground is unsuitable for traditional grave burials

2. Which word would best describe the burial practice in New Orleans?
   - A   disrespectful   B   pragmatic   C   callous   D   profound

3. What does *portal* in paragraph 2 refer to?
   - A   a carriageway   B   an entrance
   - C   a picture   D   a journey

4. According to the text which statement is CORRECT?
   - A   Tombs are only opened after a "year and a day" if they are required.
   - B   Above ground burials in New Orleans ensures preservation of the body.
   - C   Many of the names on tombs in Lafayette Cemetery are in Latin.
   - D   Caskets used in Lafayette Cemetery are generally of high quality.

5. What is a suitable word to replace *interment* in paragraph 6 as used in the text?
   Write your answer on the line. _____

6. New Orleans is described as a *melting pot*. (last paragraph)
   What is meant by this description?
   - A   it portrays New Orleans' people as a homogenous populous
   - B   it indicates that racial tensions there may be high
   - C   it is a place where different peoples and cultures cohabitate
   - D   it refers to the New Orleans hot tropical climate

7. Which word is the best synonym for *deference* as used in paragraph 6?
   - A   respect   B   legal   C   medical   D   damage

8. What is suggested by the term *unlimited interment* as used in paragraph 2?
   - A   human remains finally end up as nothing more than ashes and dust
   - B   limiting the number of times a tomb can be reused
   - C   the practice of removing old names from tombs when it is emptied
   - D   using a family burial tomb for multiple interment

Lit Tip 27 – Improve your Literacy skills   **The suffix *ism***

In Lit Tip 26 you learned about Spoonerisms.
How does the the suffix *ism* affect the meaning of words? It creates nouns that:
- may be the result of an action, such as baptism, tourism
- suggest a belief or principle, such as feminism, paganism, Buddhism
- indicate a feature of language, such as Spoonerism, colloquialism

Find the meaning of: ageism: _____
absenteeism: _____
Ism can be used as a word. In several dictionaries it is defined as an unspecified belief.

Understanding Year 8 Comprehension
A. Horsfield © Five Senses Education © W. Marlin

Effects of Media Violence

Whether or not exposure to media violence causes increased levels of aggression and violence in young people is the perennial question of media effects research. Some experts argue that fifty years of evidence show "that exposure to media violence causes children to behave more aggressively and affects them as adults years later." Others maintain that "the scientific evidence simply does not show that watching violence either produces violence in people, or desensitises them to it."

What the Researchers Are Saying

The lack of consensus about the relationship between media violence and real-world aggression has not ____(7)____ research projects. Here's a sampling of conclusions drawn from the various research strands:

Research strand: Children who consume high levels of media violence are more likely to be aggressive in the real world.

In 1956 researchers took to the laboratory to compare the behaviour of 24 children watching TV. Half watched a violent episode of the cartoon *Woody Woodpecker*, and the other 12 watched the non-violent cartoon *The Little Red Hen.* During play afterwards, the researchers observed that the children who watched the violent cartoon were much more likely to hit other children and break toys.

Six years later, in 1963, other researchers studied the effect of exposure to real-world violence, television violence, and cartoon violence. They divided 100 preschool children into four groups. The first group watched a real person shout insults at an inflatable doll while hitting it with a mallet. The second group watched the incident on television. The third watched a cartoon version of the same scene, and the fourth watched nothing.

When all the children were later exposed to a frustrating situation, the first three groups responded with more aggression than the control group. The children who watched the incident on television were slightly less aggressive to those who had watched the real person use the mallet; and both were more aggressive than those who had only watched the cartoon.

Over the years, laboratory experiments such as these, have consistently shown that exposure to violence is associated with increased heartbeat, blood pressure and respiration rate, and a greater willingness to inflict pain or punishment on others. However, this line of enquiry has been criticised because of its focus on short term results and the artificial nature of the viewing environment.

Adapted from:http://www.media-awareness.ca/english/issues/violence/effects_media_violence.cfm

Understanding discussions

Circle a letter to answer questions 1 to 8.

1. The two concerns of some researchers is that media violence can produce violent people or
   - A condition them to become involved in felonies
   - B increase scepticism of the authenticity of real life violence on TV
   - C make them less shocked or distressed by real violence
   - D satisfy viewers' deep primeval impulses

2. The 1963 research studied the reaction of three groups which were exposed to violence. What is the order from **most** influenced to **least** influenced of the groups to violence?
   - A TV violence, real world violence, cartoon violence
   - B TV violence, cartoon violence, real world violence
   - C real world violence, TV violence, cartoon violence
   - D real world violence, cartoon violence, TV violence

3. What is considered **not** to be an effect in children watching TV violence?
   - A increased heartbeat
   - B changes in breathing
   - C heightened blood pressure
   - D dilation of eye pupils

4. A criticism of much of the research regarding children and media violence is that it doesn't
   - A look into long term effects
   - B consider the amount of TV violence
   - C correlate violence to the number of cartoons watched
   - D evaluate the quality of simulated violence

5. The tone of the text tends to suggest that research will be
   - A intermittent
   - B on going
   - C abandoned
   - D conclusive

6. Which statement on the effect of media violence on children is CORRECT?
   - A There has been insufficient time given to research.
   - B The issue continues to be controversial.
   - C The inclusion of control groups add little to any data base.
   - D Vested interests have impinged upon the validity of results.

7. A word has been deleted from the text.
   Which word would be best suited to the space (7)?
   - A encouraged
   - B banned
   - C distorted
   - D impeded

8. The results of media violence research as discussed in the text would be most consequential to
   - A parents of young children
   - B producers of TV cartoons
   - C law enforcement agencies
   - D children's play-group supervisors

Lit Tip 28 – Improve your Literacy skills   *i.e.* or *e.g.?*

The term i.e. is a shortening of the Latin expression id est which translates to *that is*.
Example: He likes citrus, i.e. those juicy fruits with yellow or orange skin.

The term e.g. is a shortening of the Latin expression exempli gratia which translates to *for example*. Dad likes his greens, e.g. lettuce and rocket.

Note: According to the Australian Style Manual a stop follows each letter. Commas only precede the abbreviations.

Do not use these abbreviations in formal writing.

Understanding Year 8 Comprehension
A. Horsfield © Five Senses Education © W. Marlin

Read the article on *Natural Gemstones, Unnatural Names.*

Natural Gemstones, Unnatural Names

The world of gemstones has one foot in the technical world of mineralogy and one foot in the commercial world of jewellery. So it's not surprising that it has a mix of strange and unusual names and ordinary and familiar ones. The strange and unusual ones are hard to remember and, in many cases, even harder to spell. But it's surprising how often the familiar ones are misspelled as well.

Some of the misspellings we see are really just variants, and whether they are misspelling or not depends on where you learned your English. In Australia, UK and Canada the science of gemstones is known as gemmology. In the US it is known as gemology. Similarly, for colour and color, and facetted and faceted. Some variants are perhaps not even regional, but 'jems' and 'jemstones' are always wrong.

The most common misspelling of a gemstone term is of a long and difficult word originating in Sri Lanka. The English rendering of the Sinhalese word for lotus blossom is *padparadscha*. You'll find many incorrect variants of it, including 'padparadsha', 'padparascha', 'padparacha' and 'padparasha', You can't really blame anyone for misspelling that mouthful of syllables.

Another foreign term for a rare and valuable kind of tourmaline is the next most frequently misspelled term. Paraiba is the name for a type of copper-bearing tourmaline first found in the state of Paraiba in Brazil. The word is short and fairly easy to pronounce. But it is nonetheless frequently misspelled as 'Pariba' or 'Pariaba' tourmaline. You'll sometimes see 'Paraiba topaz' as well. The spelling is correct, but there is no such thing as Paraiba topaz!

Many English speakers seem to have trouble with gemstone terms that have foreign origins. The term for a stone cut with a highly polished rounded or convex top with no faceting, comes from the French 'caboche,' meaning small dome. The correct spelling is cabochon. We frequently see it misspelled as 'cabachon'. Or some writers try to make it more French, and spell it 'cabouchon'. Marquise, referring to an elongated oval shape with points on both ends, is often spelled 'marqui' and 'marquis'.

 Even some of the most familiar gemstone names are misspelled more often that one would expect. We often see 'blue saphire' and 'star saphire' (sapphire). You wouldn't think many people would misspell diamond, but we see 'dimond', 'daimond' and 'diamon'!

Reprinted and adapted with kind permission from SETT Company Ltd. Natural Gemstones, Unnatural Names 2014

Understanding articles

Circle a letter or write an answer for questions 1 to 8.

1. What does the writer find surprising?
   A   the wide range of unusually named gemstones
   B   the origin of the names of familiar gemstones
   C   many gemstones names are incorrectly spelled
   D   how people mispronounce the names of common gemstones

2. The article is most likely intended to
   A   educate readers who buy gems   B   entertain readers with odd facts
   C   warn readers of misnamed gemstones   D   improve readers' spelling

3. What does *faceted* in paragraph 2 refer to in gemmology?
   A   having many sides   B   the depth of colour
   C   the reflective character   D   relative weight and density

4. What is it about *Paraiba topaz* that attracted the writer's attention?
   A   it is incorrectly spelled and wrongly named
   B   it is correctly spelled and correctly named
   C   both words are misspelled
   D   it is correctly spelled but wrongly named

5. What is the correct spelling for the stone
   that is frequently used in an engagement ring?
   (It is also the stone for a sixtieth anniversary.) Write your answer here. _____

6. The name of the stone called *cabochon* has its origin in the
   A   place name from where it is found   B   soft colour embedded in its shape
   C   dome-shaped upper surface   D   mineral composition of the stone

7. According to the text which variant of the word is correctly spelled?
   A   padparasha   B   padparadscha   C   padparacha   D   padparascha

8. According to the text gemstones have two distinct interest areas for people. They are
   A   fossicking and collecting   B   investment and relationships
   C   fashion and finance   D   mineralogy and jewellery

Lit Tip 29 – Improve your Literacy skills   **People from other worlds**

Improving your word power.

Earth is the only planet that has intelligent life. People living on Earth are Earthlings.

Beings (creatures) from other plants have different names. They exist only in science fiction.

Mercury / Mercurians   Venus/ Venusians   Mars / Martians

A being from Jupiter is called _____, from Uranus _____
(Some of these words may not be in standard dictionaries.)

Beings from planets other than Earth would be termed **aliens** in science fiction.
In fact, an alien can be someone who is not a citizen of the country in which they are living.

Understanding Year 8 Comprehension
A. Horsfield © Five Senses Education © W. Marlin

Centrepoint

Even after many years, and in the safety of a provincial city, old habits die hard.

James scanned the faces of the few shoppers strolling through Centrepoint. Those that weren't directly observable were checked in the windows of the shops. Subconsciously, after years of practice, gaits and body shapes were observed.

A movement in the reflections on the silver sugar bowl attracted his attention.

'Hello. Would you like a pot of English Breakfast or something else this time?'

James turned his head to face the waitress.

Late forties, slim but not thin, attractive face with short, almost silver hair; distinctive hazel eyes that had an amused sparkle.

Time to change his pattern flashed through his mind.

'Thank you. Yes.'

'And anything to eat with that?' No notebook; this was someone who paid attention and remembered.

'No, thank you.' There was a very brief pause and a change in the eyes before the waitress responded.

'Right; be with you soon.' She turned and went to the minute kitchen that somehow managed to service the upstairs café.

Damn it! James thought. He particularly enjoyed coming to this particular café because the service was polite and efficient (which was all too rare) but not over-friendly (which was obtrusive to someone of his nature). The tea and coffee were good too. It also afforded him a degree of privacy, being above the sundry shoppers and workers that drifted through the shopping centre. He'd read, when a child, an account by Winston Churchill of lying on a high wall and noticing that few people looked up. That and his own experience had shown this to be true. The café and shopping centre also offered four quick exits and two lifts should it be necessary to leave quickly, although that seemed unlikely.

'Excuse me.' The waitress had approached him without his noticing. His smile hid the expletive that went through his mind. James moved back a little so that the tiny tray with the teapot, cup and saucer and milk jug on it could be placed on the small table.

After placing the tray on the table, the waitress stood and hesitated. 'Are you sure you wouldn't like something to eat?'

She obviously would remember him, and she wanted to initiate some kind of relationship. James had been avoiding this type of situation for over a year: anonymity was camouflage, invisibility. This would be his last visit to this café.

'Thank you but no; the tea is enough.' Voice and face neutral, no rebuff, no invitation.

Our thanks to John Andrews for permission to reprint this extract from an unpublished book Centrepoint.

Understanding narratives

1. The action of the text takes place in
   - A a shopping mall
   - B a railway station
   - C a busy street
   - D a commercial office

2. James's actions and behaviour suggest that he is
   - A on the trail of someone
   - B wanted by store security
   - C afraid of being recognised
   - D under surveillance

3. From information in the text what is a reasonable prediction of events in the narrative?
   - A someone would look up and notice James sitting in the cafe
   - B law enforcement officers will arrive to take James into custody
   - C the waitress will report James to authorities
   - D James will cease coming to that café for his cups of tea

4. James observes the *gaits* (paragraph 2) of people. What is James observing?
   - A a person's behaviour
   - B a person's manner of walking
   - C a person's ethnicity
   - D a person's racial colourings

5. How did James's reaction to the waitress evolve throughout the text?
   - A impressiveness followed by embarrassment
   - B suspicion followed by alarm
   - C hesitancy followed by openness
   - D wariness followed by annoyance

6. What action of the waitress indicated to James that she would remember him?
   - A she silently watched James's reflection in the silver sugar bowl
   - B she checked her notebook to confirm James's order preferences
   - C James's ordering routine was becoming predictable
   - D James's lack of friendliness attracted attention

7. Which word best describes James's actions and behaviour?
   - A surreptitious
   - B vigilant
   - C clandestine
   - D undercover

8. What did James find disconcerting about the café?
   - A the attentiveness of the waitress
   - B the quality of the service and the tea
   - C its high, exposed location
   - D its lack of quick convenient exits

Lit Tip 30 – Improve your Literacy skills   **Comparative adjectives**

When adjectives are used to compare two things you add er to the adjective: cool / cooler.
If three or more things are compared you add *est* to the adjective: fast / fastest
For multi-syllable words you use *more* (or less) or *most* (or least).

Examples: more (less) attractive / most (least) attractive

Irregular adjectives do not follow these patterns: far, further, furthest
Complete this table:

Base word	Comparative form	Superlative form
good	_____	_____
bad	_____	_____
many	_____	_____

Understanding Year 8 Comprehension
A. Horsfield © Five Senses Education © W. Marlin

How to play quoits

Quoits (koits, kwoits, kwaits) is a traditional game which involves the throwing of metal, rope or rubber rings over a set distance, usually to land over a spike (sometimes called a hob, peg, mott or pin).

Quoits can be played socially almost anywhere and by almost anyone. Quoit clubs have had players in their eighties. Children can join in matches. Whole families can play and the set up cost is very low. Matches can be for singles or for teams.

All you need is:
- A set of 6 quoits
- A peg
- Toeblock
- Backdrop

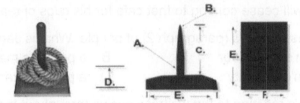

The standard peg size is (A) 3.28 cm to (B) 0.95 cm tapered over (C) 27.95 cm.
The base of the block must be (D) 7.62 cm thick.
The block size is (E) 38 cm by (F) 22.75 cm.
The throwing distance is 2.74 m from the centre of the peg to toeblock (a board on the ground, over which the thrower must not step.)
Quoit diameters are between 10.75 cm and 11.45 cm.
Quoit weight is between 170 grams and 255 grams.

Rules of the Game
Quoits are thrown directly at the peg one at a time from a set distance from alternate ends after each team has had a throw. Scoring can be a progressive tally or points for a win.

Some Common Terms
- Break: Number of quoits thrown without missing
- Possible: Maximum quoits thrown in a game without missing.
- Unfinished throw: The player throwing last in the competition stops throwing after passing opponents score.

Did You Know?
Quoits was played extensively throughout Britain in the 15th century and was enjoyed by early settlers in Australian mining communities.
The Australian Rope Quoits Council was formed in 1947 as the controlling body and to standardise equipment and rules.

There are no set standards for deck quoits - partly because of its informal nature and partly because the game has to adapt to the shape and area of the ship's deck. There are two "ends" each with a target, pegs are not used on ships, instead there is a mark painted on the deck which is referred to as a 'jack'.

World Record: A throw of 4002 unfinished by Bill Irby of Melbourne in 1967. Bill Irby passed away January 1983 and had held the Australian Open Singles Championships 6 times from 1967 to 1982.

Adapted from: http://www.jjsoz.com.au/quoits/how_to_play.html; https://en.wikipedia.org/wiki/Quoits, http://www.mastersgames.com/rules/quoits-outdoor-rules.htm

Understanding instructions

Circle a letter or write an answer for questions 1 to 8.

1. What is meant by the term *break* when playing quoits?
   - A   it is the total number of quoits thrown without a miss
   - B   it is a change of thrower when playing in teams
   - C   it is the time between the end of one match and the start of the next
   - D   it is when the leadership of a game is ceded to the opposing team

2. What event took place in 1947?
   - A   quoits was introduced into mining communities
   - B   Billy Irby had his record breaking throw
   - C   the first Australian governing body for quoits was established
   - D   Billy Irby won his first Open Singles Championship

3. What is the metric size of the area covered by the base of the peg block?

   Write your answer in the spaces.   _____ by _____

4. According to the text quoit rings are **not** made of
   - A   rope   B   steel   C   wood   D   rubber

5. The spike over which a quoit throw is directed can also be called
   - A   a needle   B   a jack   C   an end   D   a mott

6. According to the text which statement is CORRECT?
   - A   Quoits can be adapted to a wide variety of situations.
   - B   Quoits are intended for professional players.
   - C   Quoits requires a high level of physical fitness.
   - D   Quoits is a recently modern game.

7. In paragraph 2 the writer refers to people in their *eighties*.
   In this context *eighties* could also be recorded as
   - A   80's   B   80s   C   80s'   D   80S

8. What determines the size of a quoits playing space on a ship?
   - A   the speed of the ship   B   the age of the players
   - C   the cost of equipment   D   the deck space available

---

Lit Tip 31 – Improve your Literacy skills   *made from OR made of*

We use ***made of*** when we talk about the basic material or qualities of something. It has a meaning similar to *composed of*. Max's shirts were *made of* silk.

We often use ***made from*** when we talk about how something is manufactured. Pacific Islanders canoes were *made from* tree trunks.

Read: *The chair is made of wood* as wood is still seen in the environment but the cheese is made from milk because cheese is a solid produced from milk (a liquid).

Complete these sentences with *of* or *from*.

1. Stew is made _____ meat, onions and carrots.   2. Ice cream is made _____ milk.

Understanding Year 8 Comprehension
A. Horsfield © Five Senses Education © W. Marlin

Cormorant

The king of his castle
a cormorant sits motionless
on a solitary mound of mossy rock
then <u>precisely</u> spreads each of his wings
like a flamenco dancer
opening a lacy black fan

Catching the sun's golden warmth
he is the subject of a seascape
illuminated in the foreground
In the background
a yacht mimics the bird
as its sails unfurl and flap in the breeze

At the horizon bruised clouds congeal
slowly transfusing the harbour
with dark, menacing shadows
As the wind whips up and begins to wail
myriad insects frenzy on the shore
sensing the imminence of rain

Drops pummel the water
scattering craters across the surface
thunder roars beckoning accomplices
zig-zags of light split the sky
and hail batters the shells of ships
as the airborne bird escapes from the frame

Sheryl Persson

Our thanks to Sheryl Persson for permission to include her poem in this book.

Understanding poetry

Circle a letter or write an answer for questions 1 to 8.

1. In the first stanza of the poem, the poet suggests that the cormorant is
   A scintillating
   B complacent
   C majestic
   D resilient

2. The poet creates a visual image of the cormorant by comparing it to
   A an artist
   B a dancer
   C a rock
   D insects

3. To do something 'precisely' means to do it enthusiastically.

   Tick a box   TRUE ☐   FALSE ☐

4. Which two words from the poem does the poet use to appeal to the sense of sound?
   A mossy and myriad
   B transfusing and thunder
   C flamenco and batters
   D flap and pummel

5. In the lines, *'a yacht mimics the bird / as its sails unfurl in the breeze'*, the poet uses
   A personification to describe the actions of a bird
   B a metaphor to compare the size of the bird and a boat
   C onomatopoeia to describe how a yacht was moving
   D alliteration to recreate the sound of the wind

6. According to the poet, thunder's two 'accomplices' are

   1 _____   and   2 _____

7. The poet draws on imagery associated with all of the following except
   A art
   B dance
   C blood
   D food

8. Which of these words is used as a noun by the poet?
   A sails
   B wail
   C roars
   D split

9. In *Cormorant* the poet gives the impression that she is
   A recreating the scene in a painting that impressed her
   B observing changing events in a harbour as they happen
   C recording how boats have encroached on the habitat of birds
   D reflecting on the destructive nature of coastal storms on wildlife

---

Lit Tip 32 – Improve your Literacy skills   **How to use *etc.***

Et cetera is a Latin phrase that means *and other*. It is usually shortened to *etc.*
It is used to shorten a list when there are many related things to say.

Always put a full stop after *etc.*

And etc. is wrong. It means *and and others* which doesn't make much sense!

If *etc.* appears within the sentence it has a comma before and after the *etc.* - Basketball tennis, etc., are popular games. The reader (listener) will add more examples to supplement the list.

A warning: Don't use etc. in an attempt to trick the reader into thinking there are more examples than you have given or able to give!

Understanding Year 8 Comprehension
A. Horsfield © Five Senses Education © W. Marlin

Coal and Coal Seam Gas

At this most critical point in the fight against climate change, it is vital that Australia makes a just transition away from fossil fuels towards renewable energy. However, the fight for change in our mining and energy industries is ongoing. A concerted expansion of coal mining for domestic use is underway. Eleven new coal fired power plants are currently on the table across Australia.

Meanwhile, Australian coal exports are set to double over the next 10-15 years. Coal exports currently contribute 1.2 times the greenhouse gas emissions that are currently emitted within Australia's borders. Expansion plans for Queensland coal exports alone will emit an additional 460 million tonnes of carbon dioxide (CO_2) into the atmosphere per year. This is equivalent to the annual emissions of 65 average coal-fired power stations.

The explosion of coal-seam gas (CSG) exploration is putting the health and livelihoods of local communities at risk across Australia, from the Darling Downs (QLD) to central Sydney. CSG drilling puts the community at risk via leakage of methane and other toxic substances, contamination of fresh water aquifers, chemical residues from the fracking process, and increased salinity in water supplies which effect agricultural productivity.

Claims to reductions in greenhouse gas emissions from gas are flawed. While proponents insist that gas emits 70% of that emitted from coal, this calculation neglects emissions from the drilling, fracking, compressing, pumping, liquefying and transporting of the gas; nor does it account for the loss of carbon-storing forests and woodlands cleared to make way for gas wells and pipes.

Friends of the Earth (FoE) is part of the struggle against coal and coal-seam gas expansion in Australia. FoE Melbourne was involved in the successful fight to stop the HRL (an energy company) plant approval and is working with 25+ communities across the state to oppose new coal and gas proposals. FoE Brisbane has both coal and coal-seam gas campaigns. They are active in the Lock the Gate Alliance which is a network of over 110 groups around Australia that have locked their gates against coal and coal seam gas mining companies, and embarked on a campaign of non-cooperation. Another collective in Brisbane is resisting expansion of coal exports and coal mining on prime agricultural land.

FoE joined with a range of farming groups to establish Lock the Gate Alliance which has turned into a major network of local groups.

GET INVOLVED!

Sources: http://www.brisbanetimes.com.au/environment/csg-a-threat-to-us-all-20110530-1fchj.html
https://www.foe.org.au/coal-coal-seam-gas

1. How does the writer feel about the use of fossil fuels?
The writer
   A   believes benefits from fossil fuels outweigh benefits from renewable energy
   B   is confident agriculture and fossil fuel interests can co-exist
   C   accepts that the development of fossil fuel deposits is inevitable
   D   opposes further development of fossil fuel production

2. The arguments in the text relating to Coal Seam Gas could best be described as
   A   deceptively objective   B   unreasonably forceful
   C   openly one-sided   D   blatantly fanciful

3. The word *explosion* as used in paragraph 3 is an example of a
   A   a hyperbole   B   a factual observation
   C   a simile   D   an onomatopoeia

4. The *anti-coal seam gas* program is a program based upon
   A   mobilising covert dissent   B   informing the public of their options
   C   instigating legal proceedings D   lobbying for political support

5. Some experts believe the figures given by the supporters of fossil fuels are flawed because they
   A   disregard the output from suburban enterprises
   B   emphasise production predominately from Queensland
   C   ignore the benefits to workers in rural areas
   D   do not take into account activities associated with mining

6. What is a synonym for the word *proponents* as used in paragraph 4?
   A   presenters   B   investors   C   advocates   D   opponents

7. The Lock the Gate movement is most applicable to
   A   agriculturists   B   town residents
   C   exporters   D   waterside workers

8. Which of the following does the writer fear is the most environmentally unacceptable?
   A   power stations   B   fracking for CSG
   C   fossil fuel shipping   D   loss of carbon-storing forests

---

Lit Tip 33 – Improve your Literacy skills   **The suffix *cide***

The suffix cide has something to do with killing or being killed.

Homi<u>cide</u> refers to the killing of one person by another.

Here are some cide words and who/what they refer to.

suicide (oneself)   pesticide (pests)   weedicide (weeds)   patricide (one's father)
fungicide (fungus)   fratricide (a brother)   algicide (algae)   matricide (one's mother)

Who/what is killed?

regicide (_____)   genocide (_____)   germicide (_____)

Know the difference.

Murder is premeditated killing of a person.

Manslaughter is the killing of a person being without malice or planning. Both are homicides.

One Touch could be Fatal

What is ABL?
Australian Bat Lyssavirus (ABL) was first discovered in a flying fox in NSW in 1996. ABL is closely related to rabies virus. Since the 1990s, three people have died after being bitten by bats infected with ABL in Australia. All were in Queensland. It has to be assumed that ABL infection is always fatal.

How do humans get ABL?
ABL occurs in the saliva of infected bats. If a bat bites or scratches a person, saliva - and with it ABL - may be introduced into the wound. (Saliva may be on the claws of the animal as a result of grooming or licking itself.)
Regardless of the severity of the bite or scratch there is always the very high risk of infection.
There is no known risk of contracting ABL from bats flying overhead, contact with bat urine or faeces, or from fruit they may have eaten.

What species of bats are affected?
In Australia ABL has been detected in all four species of flying foxes, and at least three species of insectivorous bats.
Although very few healthy bats are infected with ABL about 5% of the sick or unwell bats that have been tested in Queensland were infected with ABL.
ABL in bats is widely distributed throughout Australia.

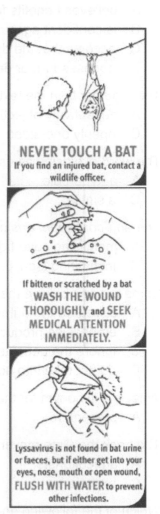

NEVER TOUCH A BAT
If you find an injured bat, contact a wildlife officer.

If bitten or scratched by a bat
WASH THE WOUND
THOROUGHLY and SEEK
MEDICAL ATTENTION
IMMEDIATELY.

Lyssavirus is not found in bat urine or faeces, but if either get into your eyes, nose, mouth or open wound, FLUSH WITH WATER to prevent other infections.

How do I know if a bat has ABL?
You can't tell from looking at a bat. A bat behaving abnormally may suggest it has ABL, but bats that appear well have also tested positive for the virus. Scientific tests on animals are the only means of determining if a bat is ABL infected.

Are any other animals able to carry ABL?
For a long timethere was no evidence that other animals including <u>domestic</u> animals and pets could be infected with ABL. However, in 2014 there were two cases of ABL in horses which has highlighted the need for greater awareness of the disease in domestic animals. The spill over to horses indicates that animals other than bats can pose
(6)   human health threats.

Precautions
You are advised not to touch bats, especially if they are distressed, injured or sick. Do not attempt to free a bat caught in a fence or a net. Contact an experienced animal handler to removed distressed or injured bats. Wildlife service can assist. Although ABL probably does not survive once a bat has died, do not handle dead bats.

It is strongly recommended that members of the public do not handle bats.

Sources: http://www.ava.com.au/node/27046,Queensland Government Tropical Public Health Services
http://www.smh.com.au/environment/animals/boys-tragic-death-serves-as-warning-to-others-20130321-2giom.html.

Understanding information reports

Circle a letter or write an answer for questions 1 to 8.

1. A scratch or bite from a bat infected with Lyssavirus
   A will most likely result in an early death
   B should be cleaned immediately
   C requires medical attention
   D has the potential to cause abnormal behaviour

2. What is the most likely source human infection of Australian Bat Lyssavirus (ABL) from bats comes from
   A bat urine   B bat saliva
   C bat carcasses   D bat faeces

3. The information in this text would ne most useful for
   A farmers   B doctors   C veterinarians   D jockeys

4. The tone of the text suggests that the writer is
   A understating the problem   B being informal and chatty
   C being forcefully direct   D promoting anxiety and stress

5. According to the text which statement is CORRECT?
   A Minor bites and scratches from bats are of little concern.
   B Bats with Lyssavirus are easily identified.
   C Bats caught in nets or trapped on fences will carry Lyssavirus.
   D Fruit that has been eaten by bats does not pose an ABL health risk.

6. A word has been deleted from the text.
   Which word would be best suited to the space (6)?
   A dormant   B potential   C nominal   D negligible

7. Which is the best **antonym** for *domestic* as used in the subsection **Are any other animals able to carry ABL?**
   A free   B feral   C untrained   D wild

8. The graphics and much of the information in this text came from an information brochure.
   Where would be a suitable place to make this brochure available to the public?
   A the waiting room of a medical centre in a bat habitat region
   B the reception office of a police station in a bat habitat region
   C a wildlife care and recovery centre in a bat habitat region
   D any school library in a bat habitat region

Lit Tip 34 – Improve your Literacy skills   **When to use an asterisk (*)**

The **asterisk** is the small star symbol which can be used to indicate a footnote or used to edit blashemies or expletives — and sometimes names of actual people — in a text.

Footnotes conventionally begin on the bottom of the page on which the asterisk occurs. Using the asterisk as a footnote symbol shows that you plan to comment on something in the text.

The asterisk is a strategy of showing swear words without offending the reader. Can you work out what this word is? d**n. They are often used in cartoons and comics. As with many literary ploys do not over use them in your writing.

In maths an asterisk represents a multiplication symbol: 3 * 5 = 15

Understanding Year 8 Comprehension
A. Horsfield © Five Senses Education © W. Marlin

Read the extract *Glenridge Bargain.*

Glenridge Bargain

They cruised slowly through Glenridge as unobtrusively as possible. Suddenly Garth pointed. 'There!'

'What?'

'On the nature strip.'

Trevor braked and reversed the ute until they were adjacent a grey Holden Sandman panel van, standing in a bed of dried grass spikes. A faded red FOR SALE sign was propped at an awkward angle inside the windscreen. In hand written black-marker at the bottom of the sign were the words, '$1950 apply within'. Trevor got out for a closer look.

The vehicle had clearly been a workhorse for a number of years but it was unlikely to attract police attention for a road-worthy check. Clean, no obvious rust, still had enough tread on the tyres, only a couple of short scrapes on the passenger's side and a ding in the rear door. The rear vision mirrors were in place and the windscreen had no obvious wiper arc scratches.

An old man was watching them without moving from a veranda.

Trevor got back into the ute and drove it into the first side street. About five hundred metres down the street he found a house with a tired Real Estate agent's FOR SALE sign on the front lawn which hadn't been mown for weeks. The place looked empty and neglected. Paper, stained plastic and drink containers had collected in struggling shrubs and accumulated in small messy piles along the fence line. No gates, just spaces.

Trevor drove the ute into an empty, dusty carport beside the house, pulled out the 'For Sale' sign and tossed onto the back of the ute.

Without looking back they headed to the main road and the panel van. They walked around it and peered in the windows. Garth tested a door.

'Locked,' said the old man laconically as he pushed open a gate that scrapped across the gravel. 'Take the shirt off yer back some of <u>them</u>.'

Garth raised his eyes quickly at Trevor.

'No time for <u>tyre kickers</u>.'

Trevor nodded at the old man. 'Been after one of these.'

Garth swung into action. 'One owner?'

The old man gave a tight smile. 'Had her since I came to Glenridge. Serviced by my mate down the street. Never driven more than a few thousand ks each year.'

'Fifteen-hundred cash?' offered Trevor slickly. 'But a test drive first.'

'Where's yer ute?' the old man asked suspiciously.

From an idea in Two-way Cut by Garry Disher, ebook version.

Understanding narratives

Circle a letter or write an answer for questions 1 to 8.

1. Trevor and Garth are heading somewhere. It is quite likely they are
   - A going on a holiday
   - B looking for employment
   - C running from personal strife
   - D shopping for a new car

2. The old man says: *take the shirt off yer back some of them*.
   Who does the *them* most likely refer to?
   - A vandals
   - B thieves
   - C burglars
   - D teenagers

3. Which of the two men is most likely the leader?
   Write your answer on the line. _____

4. The old man became suspicious when
   - A Trevor kicked the tyres of his van
   - B he was was offered a cash sale well below the listed price
   - C he saw Garth trying a car door handle
   - D Garth and Trevor returned to the Sandman on foot

5. As used in the text, which is the best definition of a *tyre kicker*?
   A *tyre kicker* is a person who
   - A inspects goods without any intention of buying
   - B has a respectable knowledge of a car's condition
   - C is readily angered if that person finds an item he cannot obtain
   - D intends to buy an item cheaply for a quick resale and profit

6. In which order did the events in the Glenridge episode occur?
   - **1.** Trevor find a disused garage for his ute
   - **2.** Garth tries to open a door of the Sandman
   - **3.** Garth recognises a vehicle for sale
   - **4.** Trevor discovers an abandoned house

   - A 3, 2, 1, 4
   - B 4, 1, 2, 3
   - C 3, 4, 1, 2
   - D 2, 3, 1, 4

7. Which word would best describe Trevor's behaviour?
   - A devious
   - B sinister
   - C impractical
   - D menacing

8. A suitable alternate title for the passage would be
   - A The Locked Sandman
   - B A Plan Change
   - C House for Sale
   - D Danger for an Old Man

Lit Tip 35 – Improve your Literacy skills   Compound nouns

A compound noun contains two or more words which join together to make a simple noun.
Compound nouns can be words written together (clubhouse), words that are hyphenated (father-in-law) or separate words that go together by meaning (bus stop).

The words that form a compound noun can be two nouns (firefly), adjective and noun (blackberry), noun and verb (sunrise), verb and preposition (checkout), preposition and noun (underground) and noun and adjective (handful).

To do: Underline four compound nouns in the text Glenridge Bargain.

Understanding Year 8 Comprehension
A. Horsfield © Five Senses Education © W. Marlin

The Lighthouse

36

Read the description *The Lighthouse.*

The Lighthouse

The small group waited for the speaker to start. She gave a gentle cough.

'Rocky Point Lighthouse was designed by the famous architect Edmund Greenly in 1832 and was built of granite and sandstone. It is an octagonal lighthouse with a base that is wider than the top. It has a modest tapering.

'Originally an open coal fire was used for lighting in the 1840s. The lighthouse keeper had to carry bags of coal up the steep internal stairwell. Coal fire was replaced by <u>a so-called an improved lens</u> using oil lamps. In 1891 a kerosene lamp was introduced. This was combined with a shutter system which made it possible to produce different signals for weather information and shipping lanes.

'The lighthouse beacon was turned off in 1953 when a more sophisticated facility was built on Henderson Heads at the entrance to the archipelago. This one was completely renovated in the 1980s with government funding which included the installation of an appealing <u>dim orange light</u>. There's life in the <u>old girl</u> yet!

'Feel free to go in but just a few at a time. Take care. The floor and steps are a little uneven. You will find it a little damp and somewhat cooler inside. You can move up the stairs to the final landing. Do step carefully!'

The small group made its way slowly up the slightly deeper than normal stairs. From the cramped landing narrow white-painted small steps led to the lantern room. At the foot of these steps was a solid wooden door that led onto the small walkway around the tower.

The speaker pressed her way through the group, opened the door and invited the small group to move outside.

The view from the landing was extensive. It was a clear day. The sea lay spread out before them like a slightly wrinkled bed cover. The hundreds of islands and inlets strewn across the inlet was staggering. It was possible just to see the lighthouse at Henderson Heads.

Raising her voice about the slight breeze and soft hiss of the ocean the speaker said, 'Lighthouse life in the early days was a miserable, harsh existence, especially for the women. Every household task had to be carried out with neither electricity or running water. The lighthouse had to be manned 24/7 regardless of the weather and the keeper's health. And this went on year after year.

'The stone for the tower came from Nottleys Hill, five kilometres away. Only the internal section is built of sandstone from the headland nearby. You will notice that there is a darker grey ring around the top. It is most likely the final sandstone delivery didn't arrive and the mason used local rock from Devils Cove. Close and handy.

'They did all this without the equipment and tools we have available today. I think it's time were left the walkway to the gulls and make our way carefully back to the base where I will answer any questions you might have.'

Adapted from an idea in the ebook Still Waters by Viveca Sten

Understanding Year 8 Comprehension
A. Horsfield © Five Senses Education © W. Marlin   72

Understanding descriptions

Circle a letter or write an answer for questions 1 to 8.

1. For visitors their main interest in the Rocky Point Lighthouse would be its
   A architectural splendour
   B historical importance
   C cultural significance
   D photographic opportunity

2. The speaker in the passage is most likely
   A a tourist guide
   B the lighthouse keeper
   C an architect
   D a stone mason

3. The speaker says in her description *a so-called an improved lens* in paragraph 3.
   By saying this she is implying that
   A the quality of the lens was unknown
   B the lens was improved in later models
   C any assertion using improved should be doubted
   D it is a description that is commonly used

4. Which was the final feature of the lighthouse the group visited?
   A the lantern room
   B the narrow and steep stairwell
   C the cramped internal landing
   D the tower's external walkway

5. What is the most likely purpose of the dim orange light referred to in paragraph 4?
   A to guide ships through the archipelago
   B to provide lighting for lighthouse workers
   C to add an aesthetic point of interest to renovations
   D to distinguish the lighthouse from other structures in the area

6. The *old girl* referred to in paragraph 4 is
   A a female in the visiting group
   B the actual lighthouse
   C the speaker herself
   D a lighthouse keeper's wife

7. This descriptive texts relies heavily on
   A aural inputs
   B visual images
   C olfactory perceptions
   D tactile sensations

8. Write the numbers 1 to 4 in the boxes to show the correct order in which events occurred in the text.

	light from coal fires was the primary source of lighthouse illumination
	the Rocky Point beacon was turned off permanently
	the Henderson Heads lighthouse began construction
	kerosene lamps were first used at the Rocky Point Lighthouse

---

Lit Tip 36 – Improve your Literacy skills   **Compound verbs**

A **compound verb** is a verb that is made up of two or more words that function as a single verb.
Examples: colour code, outgun, air-condition, babysit, kick start, idiot proof, type set
(**Note:** Some may also act as other parts of speech.)

Underline the compound verbs:

Double click the mouse to get a result.

Tap dance your way to stardom!

They dry freeze all their vegetables before packaging.

Dad waterproofs the timber with oil.

Drop kick the ball to the sideline.

(Compound verbs may also be made with participles: was running, am willing, had played)

Understanding Year 8 Comprehension
A. Horsfield © Five Senses Education © W. Marlin

Avenue of Honour

The funeral service for Afghanistan casualty Private Benjamin Chuck held at Tinaburra on Lake Tinaroo shores outside Yungaburra township on 1 July 2010 was attended by more than 1000 people. It generated strong awareness in the local community of the service and sacrifice given by members of the Armed Forces in defence of our country and way of life.

The idea of an Avenue of Honour arose from a speech given by an <u>Ex</u> National Serviceman on Anzac Day 2010. He said, 'There should be an avenue of living trees... to represent every digger we have lost in the Afghanistan Campaign.' These words proved to be the catalyst for Benjamin Chuck's parents to begin the push for a magnificent Avenue of Honour which now serves as Australia's first living and solemn memorial to all who served in the Afghanistan Campaign.

Six years later the community had built an inspirational memorial. it is dedicated to those who served in the fight against terrorism and made the ultimate sacrifice in defence of freedom and liberty.

The thought that went into the features is moving. The intention to create a timeless, tasteful memorial of world standard has been achieved.

Photo A. Horsfield

The Entrance: The rugged rocky entrance serves as a reminder of Afghanistan's harsh landscape. The pathway is a reminder of the desert hues and desert landscape. Hand wrought sprigs of rosemary are featured in the iron art and bollards, a symbol of remembrance.

Central Memorial: This features soaring wings above a central pillar of Tarin Kot stones. The right wing is visibly damaged - a reminder that despite trials and challenges they faced the spirit of the men that served remained committed to their country and resilient to the cause.

Stones from Tarin Kot: Along with the heat and dust Afghanistan is covered in stones. Stones were carried back by survivors to form part of the central pillar as a worthy and befitting gesture to their fallen brothers.

The Journey Home: Standing at the memorial and facing the first flame tree on the right visitors are looking towards Afghanistan - 10 000 km to the north-west.

The Avenue: Flame trees border the path of fallen Commando Ben Chuck's gun carriage

and symbolises the 'final journey home' for the Fallen and preserves for ever the gratitude and respect the nation bestows on all of those it owes a debt . . . that can never be repaid. The flame tree is a native species which flowers from November through January and in full bloom on Remembrance Day representing the cycle of life. It symbolises the final journey home for the fallen.

Military Dogs: Dogs have served our country proud. They 'sniffed' out land mines. The Avenue remembers the dogs and their handlers who died or were injured in action. The memorial is also in memory of the men and women who served in the conflict and returned and continue to live with their visible and unseen wounds.

Adapted from: http://www.avenueofhonour.com.au/, private visit March 2016
Flame tree photo adapted from the above site.

Understanding explanations

1. The significance of the gun carriage as referred in the text is that it
    A   indicates the section of the armed services to which a soldier belonged
    B   is a method of recognition of the highest honours a soldier achieved
    C   signifies the belief that peace will only come through preparedness
    D   is a traditional way to transport the caskets of a soldier to his graves

2. What part did the military dogs play in the Afghanistan war?
    A   they helped guard the camps   B   they patrolled military equipment
    C   they search for and locate land mines D   they brought down enemy soldiers

3. What is the meaning of *Ex* as used in paragraph 2?
    A   unknown   B   former   C   out of   D   from

4. What is the significance of the damaged wing in the central memorial?
    A   in hazardous conditions Australian soldiers undertook great risks
    B   it recognises the great price that was paid in lives and equipment
    C   it is a symbol of bravery of those involved in flying missions
    D   in the face of adversity the servicemen remained true to their cause

5. The memorial at Tinaburra is intended to
    A   celebrate a victory   B   pay homage to Australian soldiers
    C   develop a point of interest for visitors D   glorify Australia's war successes

6. The sprigs of rosemary in the wrought iron work at the memorial represent
    A   remembrance for fallen soldiers
    B   the Afghanistan environment
    C   wounded soldiers that returned home
    D   a symbol of peace

7. Which word best reflects the feelings behind the concept of the Tinaburra memorial?
    A   admiration   B   patriotism   C   gratitude   D   heroism

8. The text states: *the nation bestows on all of those it owes a debt … that can never be <u>repaid</u>.*
   This debt cannot be *repaid* because
    A   the soldier paid for his service with his life
    B   no price can be put on eternal peace
    C   a small town does not have the resources to pay the debt
    D   money was spent on establishing the memorial

Lit Tip 37 – Improve your Literacy skills   Words from Mars

Improve your word power.

- Mars, the planet, was named after the Roman god of war.

- The month of March is named after Mars. Martians come from Mars.

- The word <u>martial</u> relates to fighting as in martial arts, martial law.

- A *court martial* is a trial for members of the military who have broken military laws.

- martially (adverb) in a war-like manner

- Martins (swallow-like birds) that arrive in some countries in March.

Understanding Year 8 Comprehension
A. Horsfield © Five Senses Education © W. Marlin

Last Cab to Darwin

(M) General release (124 minutes)

The film adapted from a stage play is based on the true-life story of cab driver Rex Bell. I saw it on an aeroplane. Its outback expanses would be more successful on a larger screen. Filming took place in remote spots such as Oodnadatta and Barrow Creek.

Last Cab to Darwin is a road trip movie through the centre of Australia.

Michael Caton's acting makes *Last Cab to Darwin* an enjoyable film. He balances the comic and the drama with ease. It is a memorable performance.

Converting a screenplay to film requires skill and it's done competently. The movie runs a leaner 124 minutes, and struggles to fully explore the issues of interracial relationships, euthanasia and alcoholism. The racism issue reflects Australian society.

Rex (Caton) has had a cancer operation before the movie opens. It was unsuccessful and he might have three months.

On the radio, he hears a Darwin doctor, Nicole Farmer (Jacki Weaver),advocating the need for right-to-die legislation. She has developed a machine that will provide assistance.

After one phone call, Rex decides to go. No waiting, no fuss. Except there are people who love him – and the one who feels for him most, his black neighbour Polly (Ningali Lawford), is his little secret, but she is hardly considered in his decisions.

Rex is a born-and-bred Broken Hill-ite. He drinks with his close mates till closing time, then staggers home to his weatherboard cottage.

Next morning, Polly brings him tea and toast from her place, after shouting abuse of his behaviour for the benefit of the nosy neighbours. Rex may hold her hand on the porch, but only when the neighbours aren't _____(6)_____.

Rex leaves quietly, after telling Polly of his decision. On the road, he picks up a young black man who's running from everything. Tilly (Mark Coles Smith) is a slick-mouthed misfit who tries to rob him, but Rex saves him from a beating by his (black) creditors. They bond in adversity, as they head north.

Along the way Julie (Emma Hamilton), an English nurse, joins the odyssey. Her compassion highlighting Rex's emotional shallowness and Dr Farmer's medico-legal inhibitions.

Caton ties the film to the outback with his dry humour and his portrayal of pain while accepting he is in his last weeks. Having never left Broken Hill, Rex now experiences a wider world, just as he's about to leave it. It's a plot worthy of its drama and <u>pathos</u>. It doesn't quite achieve its full potential but you have to respect the attempt.

Adapted from review by Phil Burns SMH 5 Aug 2015, The Cairns Post
(Kerstin Kehren) July 2015 and a personal viewing

Understanding film reviews

Circle a to answer questions 1 to 8.

1. Who played the part of the slick-mouthed misfit?
    A   Mark Coles Smith   B   Jacki Weaver
    C   Ningali Lawford   D   Emma Hamilton

2. Which issue plays only an incidental part in the film?
    A   interracial relationships   B   euthanasia
    C   alcoholism   D   remote isolation

3. Which option best describes the reviewer's response to the film?
    A   positive with reservations   B   disappointing and over-ambitious
    C   simplistic but enjoyable   D   ponderous and insensitive

4. Where is *it* the reviewer referring to in the words: *just as he's about to leave it*? (last para.)
    A   Broken Hill township   B   the Australian outback
    C   Rex's life on Earth   D   the Darwin doctor's premises

5. What is the most likely reason Rex keeps his affection for Polly secret?
    A   he is an alcoholic who has difficulty expressing his emotions
    B   he feels that his friendship will not be understood in a racist environment
    C   because of his age he suspects he will be regarded as an amusement
    D   she is the only person he trusts with his cancer plans

6. A word has been deleted from the text.
    Which word would be best suited to the space (6)?
    A   annoyed   B   asleep   C   watching   D   drinking

7. Which would be a suitable synonym for *pathos* as used in the last paragraph?
    A   sadness   B   pity   C   despair   D   feebleness

8. According to the text what can be assumed is a likely outcome of Rex's trip north?
    A   he will die in Darwin while undergoing treatment
    B   he will set up a taxi company in Darwin
    C   he and Tilly will continue their journey around Australia
    D   he will return to Broken Hill and Polly

Lit Tip 38 – Improve your Literacy skills   Compound adjectives

Compound adjectives are formed when two or more words are joined to modify the same noun: red-hot (metal), cold-blooded (act), south-west (wind), blue-green (algae)

A hyphen is often used to hold the adjectives together, but not always: railway (line).
Can you spot the difference? 1. an old tree logging town 2. an old tree-logging town
The hyphen puts the emphasise *on tree-logging town* not on old tree logging.

One sentence has a compound verb. Highlight the compound verb in that sentence.

    1.   Before adding the meat stir-fry the vegetables.

    2.   We all had a stir-fry at the Thai café.

Highlight three compound adjectives in the film review text.

Understanding Year 8 Comprehension
A. Horsfield © Five Senses Education © W. Marlin

Discovery of Fairy Rings in Australia

Fairy rings (usually associated with toadstools) are those seemingly random patches of lifeless dirt in arid grasslands - have been a mystery to scientists and local people alike. Explanations have been numerous and diverse, including folklore suggesting they could be the work of gods or spirits - hence the name. Until recently, scientists had only seen them in Namibia, Africa.

Now, in a <u>paper</u>, scientists report that they have found them in the western Australian outback, and that they are nearly identical to those found in Namibia. Scientists are more confident that they have narrowed down the cause of these mysterious dirt patches.

Since researchers first started seeing them in Namibia, they have studied, researched, and theorised how they form. While numerous theories exist, scientists have narrowed them down into two main theories that might hold: the first puts the blame on termites. To get water, termites eat at a tree's roots in a circular pattern. That way when the water trickles down, it gets stored in the soil instead of being absorbed the roots, creating a mini reservoir the termites can access.

The other theory is known as the self-organisation theory. As it applies to nature, the idea is that as new vegetation grows, each mature tree or plant needs to be a certain distance away from another tree or plant in order to survive and thrive. As this happens, random areas of land - these fairy circles - form as a result of how the vegetation arranges itself.

The researchers found the Australian circles formed patterns very similar ■ the Namibian ones, giving more support for the self-organisation theory. They had the same hexagonal patterns.

However, while the pattern is the same, they function in different ways in each location. The area in Australia where the fairy circles are abundant doesn't get regular rainfall. So as trees grow, their roots grow longer to collect the water. As that happens, the roots loosen the soil around them, making plants closer to the large tree easier to grow and plants farther away less able to grow. As a result, these random areas of dry land form.

In low-rainfall Namibia the circles act as troughs that then store and provide water to the thirsty plants and trees that surround it.

To test the termite theory Australian researchers used GPS to map the termites and ants in the areas in and surrounding the fairy circles, and found no correlation between the two.

This Australian discovery may indicate that fairy circles may occur in other locations.

Adapted from: http://www.popsci.com.au/science/nature/discovery-of-fairy-circles-in-australia-helps-scientists-pinpoint-their-mysterious-origins,416965, Claire Maldarelli

Understanding recounts

Circle a letter to answer questions 1 to 8.

1. The self-organisation theory refers to the concept that
   A termites move into areas to deplete plant life around established trees
   B mature trees need to be a certain space from other trees in order to survive
   C plants will automatically form regular patterns in dry climate environments
   D hexagonal 'rings' are the result of low rainfall and loose soil

2. One of the possible outcomes of the Australian research into fairy rings is that
   A they possibly exist in places other than Namibia and Australia
   B termites are responsible for the rings wherever they form
   C the dry patches protect underground water reserves
   D the rings from different international locations vary markedly

3. Which theory about the formation of fairy rings has the least credibility?
   A the rings resulted from termites eating the end of tree roots for moisture
   B tree roots spread in a circular pattern to collect available water
   C termites loosened the soil around nearby trees
   D they were the work of gods

4. In paragraph 2 the writer refers to a _paper._
   Which type of paper is the writer referring to?
   A a newspaper   B a personal,legal document
   C a published academic essay   D a set of test questions

5. According to the text one of these statements is **NOT** correct.
   Which statement is **NOT** correct?
   A The Namibian discoveries preceded the Australian discovery of fairy rings.
   B The formation of fairy rings had been attributed to the supernatural.
   C Plant survival strategies prevent an infestation of termites in fairy rings.
   D A GPS was used to locate termite and ant infestations.

6. It had been suggested that termites were responsible for
   A storing water underground   B denuding areas of vegetation
   C loosening the soil around trees   D eating root tips to access moisture

7. A preposition has been blacked out in paragraph. 5.
   Which would be the most suitable preposition to replaced the ■ ?
   A with   B to   C from   D of

8. Fairy rings in outback Australia
   A reappear after rain   B are spaced equidistantly
   C form in tropical locations   D are hexagonal in shape

Lit Tip 39 – Improve your Literacy skills   _High_ OR _tall_?

We use **high** when we talk about things a long way above the ground.
The switch was too high for the child to reach.
High can be used for things that have a wide base. There are some high mountains in France.
We use **tall** when we talk about people. Tall people often get backache.
We may also use tall for things high and thin (tall towers) and things that grow (trees).

Highlight the correct word.
1. The fort was built (high, tall) on the hill.   2. Jack is at least 180 cm (high, tall).
3. The factory had three (high, tall) chimneys.   4. A (tall, high) fence surrounds the jail.

Understanding Year 8 Comprehension
A. Horsfield © Five Senses Education © W. Marlin

Sir Edmund Hillary

"On 29 May 1953 a young New Zealander stood on top of Mt Everest with his climbing companion Tenzing Norgay. That young man was Edmund Hillary, soon to be knighted, and to become the most famous New Zealander of our time.

Sir Ed's achievement on that day cannot be underestimated. He went to a height and a place no man had gone before. He went there with 1950s, not 21st Century, technology. He went there with well <u>honed</u> climbing skills, developed in New Zealand, Europe, and Nepal itself. But above all, he went there with attitude – with a clear goal, with courage, and with a determination to succeed.

That attitude, Sir Ed's "can do" pragmatism, and his humility as the praise flowed for him over the decades, endeared Sir Ed to our nation and made him an inspiration and a role model for generations of New Zealanders.

Today we all mourn with Lady Hillary, with Peter and Sarah and all Sir Ed's extended family, knowing that their loss is personal and profound, and valuing their willingness to share this farewell with us all. We mourn as a nation. We know we are saying goodbye to a friend.

Whether we knew Sir Ed personally a lot, a little, or not at all, he was a central part of our New Zealand family. My parents' and grandparents' generation followed Ed's adventures. Those of us who cannot remember the news of that great climb grew up knowing of the man and the legend, as today's children do.

And how privileged we were to have that living legend with us for eighty-eight years. Prior to Sir Ed's conquest of Everest, the mountain had defeated fifteen previous expeditions. Reaching the summit was considered one of our world's last great challenges.

So when the news broke of the ascent by Ed Hillary, a beekeeper from New Zealand, and Tenzing Norgay, a Sherpa from Nepal, it made headlines around the world. This was one of the defining moments of the twentieth century, and earned these two brave men their place in history. There then followed many other achievements of note.

Earlier this month, the fiftieth anniversary was observed of Sir Ed's journey to the South Pole - when he became the first person to make the land crossing since Amundsen and Scott. In Kiwi style, Sir Ed did the crossing on a tractor.

We loved Sir Ed for what he represented – a determination to succeed against the odds, humility, an innate sense of fair play, and a tremendous sense of service to the community, at home and abroad.

As individuals, we may not be able to match Sir Ed's abilities or strength, but we can all strive to match his humanity and compassion for others.

His values were strong; they are timeless; and they will endure.
May Sir Edmund Hillary rest in peace."

(Sir Edmund Hillary's Eulogy presented by Helen Clark, New Zealand Prime Minister 2008)
Adapted from: https://www.funeralwise.com/plan/eulogy/hillary/

Understanding eulogies

Circle a letter or write an answer for questions 1 to 8.

1. How old was Sir Edmund Hillary when he died?
   Write your answer on the line _____

2. Which option best describes a eulogy?
   - A a speech that praises someone highly who has just died
   - B a ceremony of religious worship according to a prescribed form for the deceased
   - C a public recount of a person's life and times after they have died
   - D a historical account given from a deep personal association with a dead person

3. According to PM Clark, which attribute did not figure in Sir Edmund Hillary's achievement?
   - A having a clear, defined goal
   - B an attitude of pragmatism
   - C a trust in God
   - D a determination to succeed

4. A fitting title for the text would be
   - A The Everest Challenge
   - B Sorrowful Hearts
   - C Tenzing Norgay and Edmund Hillary
   - D A Hero for all New Zealanders

5. Which aspect of Sir Edmund's life did Helen Clark find somewhat unorthodox?
   - A being a New Zealand bee-keeper
   - B driving a tractor to cross Antarctica
   - C using a Nepalese guide on his Everest climb
   - D climbing Mt Everest without modern technology

6. The tone of Helen Clark's eulogy is
   - A ritualistic and affected
   - B informal and rambling
   - C inspirational and cordial
   - D pompous and official

7. As used in the text, a *honed* skill (paragraph 2) is one that
   - A is repeatedly practised
   - B develops over many years
   - C arises from outdoor labour
   - D is refined to perfection

8. When Sir Edmund 'conquered' Mt Everest Helen Clark would have been a
   - A young person
   - B grandparent
   - C prime minister of New Zealand
   - D friend of the Hillary family

Lit Tip 40 – Improve your Literacy skills **Word oddities**

This is a challenge and just for fun!

These words all have a similar characteristic. Can you spot what the characteristic is?

banana, dresser, grammar, potato, revive, uneven, assess.

Clue 1: It has nothing to do with their meanings.

Some more words: solo, rococo, moo, belle, brer, tutu, bee, lotto, revive, prefer

Clue 2: A palindrome is a word that can be spelled forwards and backwards. Look for a section of each word that is palindromic.

Clue 3: It also has something to do with the first letter. (explanation in Answers section)

Understanding Year 8 Comprehension
A. Horsfield © Five Senses Education © W. Marlin

SOLUTIONS

ANSWERS – Reading Comprehension Tests   84, 85

ANSWERS – Literacy Tip Exercises   86, 87

Understanding Year 8 Comprehension
A. Horsfield © Five Senses Education © W. Marlin

No.	Title	Answers

1. **Bennelong:** 1. C   2. A   3. B   4. A   5. D   6. B   7. D   8. D

2. **Life jackets:** 1. C   2. A   3. (3)   4. D   5. B   6. C   7. D   8. A

3. **Coketown:** 1. A   2. C   3. D   4. B   5. D   6. C   7. B   8. A

4. **Theia Hypothesis:** 1. D   2. C   3. B   4. D   5. C   6. D   7. A   8. B

5. **Memory:** 1. A   2. B   3. D   4. C   5. C   6. A   7. D   8. B

6. **Gympie-Gympie stinging tree:** 1. B   2. Cyril Bromley   3. A   4. B   5. A   6. D   7. C   8. D

7. **Scrounger and Charlie:** 1. C   2. A   3. B   4. D   5. C   6. A   7. B   8. Gumbo and goanna, **OR** Grinchy, the grouchy blue tongued lizard **OR** Wally the water buffalo

8. **The coconut tree legend:** 1. A   2. B   3. D   4. C   5. (2, 4, 3,1)   6. A   7. latter   8. B

9. **Are green potatoes safe?:** 1. B   2. A   3. A   4. D   5. C   6. FALSE   7. D   8. B

10. **Applying for a Job:** 1. A   2. B   3. C   4. D   5. D   6. C   7. B   8. A

11. **Wind Spirit :** 1. B   2. A   3. C   4. C   5. D   6. D   7. B   8. A

12. **Savannahlander Itinerary:** 1. B   2. A   3. C   4. D   5. B   6. D   7. 5 hr, 15 min   8. A

13. **The Hundred-Foot Journey:** 1. C   2. D   3. B   4. A   5. D   6. A   7. C   8. B

14. **What are water bears?:** 1. A   2. C   3. D   4. B   5. C   6. A   7. B   8. D

15. **The Vanilla Island:** 1. B   2. A   3. C   4. C   5. D   6. B   7. motu   8. D

16. **Space weather:** 1. B   2. B   3. C   4. D   5. A   6. D   7. C   8. A

17. **Hammerheads:** 1. A   2. C   3. B   4. D   5. D   6. C   7. D   8. A

18. **Heat Wave:** 1. D   2. B   3. A   4. C   5. A   6. D   7. B   8. A

19. **Deposit on drink containers:** 1. D   2. HIGH   3. C   4. B   5. A   6. C   7. beverage   8. A

20. **The green thing:** 1. C   2. A   3. B   4. D   5. C   6. A   7. B   8. C

Continued on the next page......

No.	Title	Answers

21. Evolution: 1. C   2. A   3. D   4. B   5. D   6. A   7. B   8. C

22. Making a Storyboard?: 1. A   2. C   3. D   4. D   5. A   6. B   7. B   8. C

23. Cannibals' Gold: 1. A   2. B   3. D   4. A   5. B   6. C   7. C   8. D

24. Spencer Williams: 1. D   2. B   3. A   4. B   5. C   6. (2, 3, 1, 4)   7. D   8. A

25. Spider-man Comic covers: 1. B   2. C   3. 1960s   4. B   5. D   6. A   7. D   8. C

26. Cobbold Gorge: 1. B   2. B   3. D   4. C   5. A   6. D   7. A   8. C

27. Burial Styles: 1. D   2. B   3. B   4. A   5. burial (or a funeral)   6. C   7. A   8. D

28. Media Violence: 1. C   2. C   3. D   4. A   5. B   6. B   7. D   8. A

29. Natural Gemstones: 1. C   2. B   3. A   4. D   5. diamond   6. C   7. B   8. D

30. Centrepoint: 1. A   2. C   3. D   4. B   5. D   6. C   7. B   8. A

31. How to play quoits: 1. A   2. C   3. 38 cm x 22.75 cm   4. C   5. D   6. A   7. B   8. D

32. Cormorant: 1. C   2. B   3. False   4. D   5. A   6. lighting and hail   7. D   8. A   9. B

33. Coal and Coal Seam Gas: 1. D   2. C   3. A   4. B   5. D   6. C   7. A   8. B

34. One Touch could be Fatal: 1. A   2. B   3. A   4. C   5. D   6. B   7. D   8. A

35. Glenridge Bargain: 1. C   2. B   3. Trevor   4. D   5. A   6. C   7. A   8. B

36. The Lighthouse: 1. B   2. A   3. C   4. D   5. C   6. B   7. B   8. (1, 3, 4, 2)

37. Avenue of Honour: 1. D   2. C   3. B   4. D   5. B   6. A   7. C   8. A

38. Last Cab to Darwin: 1. A   2. D   3. A   4. C   5. B   6. C   7. A   8. D

39. Discovery of Fairy Rings: 1. B   2. A   3. D   4. C   5. C   6. A   7. B   8. D

40. Sir Edmund Hillary: 1. 88 years   2. A   3. C   4. D   5. B   6. C   7. D   8. A

Understanding Year 8 Comprehension
A. Horsfield © Five Senses Education © W. Marlin

Year 8 Answers — Lit tips exercises

No. Text title	Topic	Answers
1. Bennelong	Life dates	No response required.
2. Life jackets	Colloquialisms or Idioms	1, 4 and 5
3. Coketown	Descriptive texts	The early dawn air was crisp and sharp as bright sunlight boldly caught the white peaks.
4. Theia Hypothesis	Correct usage: majority	plural example
5. Memory	The suffix *arian*	authoritarian, centenarian, grammarian, planetarium
6. Gympie-Gympie tree	The prefix *auto*	Suggestions: autopilot, autocrat, autosuggestion (self hypnosis) autograph (one's own), autofocus Automat: a (food) vending machine
7. Scrounger and Charlie	When to use italics	spoken responses
8. The coconut tree legend	*former* and *latter*	latter
9. Are green potatoes safe?	Starting with *And*	No response required.
10. Applying for a Job	*Effect* and *affect*	1. affect, 2. affect, 3. effect
11. Wind Spirit	Nautical terms	pork, fore, bow
12. Savannahlander Itinerary	Plural forms	JPs, POWs, 1930s
13. Hundred-Foot Journey	Mood	humdrum (lacking excitement)
14. Water bears	Morphemes	15 morphemes, 16 syllables
15. The Vanilla Island	Brackets	NRL, Royal Flying Doctor Service, OIC
16. Space weather	Interjections	Suggestions only: Hey! Ouch! Whoa!
17. Hammerheads	Noun gender	Suggestions: personal assistant, hero, singer, cowhand, host
18. Heat Wave	Prefix *para*	1. seemingly contradictory statement which when investigated may be true 2. wide parachute - like canopy attached to a person's body allowing them to glide
19. Drink containers	Modal verbs	L, H, H, H, L, L
20. The green thing	Writing the time	No response required

Continued on the next page......

No. Text title	Topic	Answers
21. Evolution	Dashes	No response required.
22. Making a Storyboard?	Hypens	man-eating shark
23. Cannibals' Gold	*And* after a comma	(The storm last night caused lines to come down), and (many people were left without power).
24. Spencer Williams	Short word forms	perambulator, newspaper, tugboat, caravan, examination, application
25. Spider-man Comic cover	prefix *super*	take the place of something/person; large grocery store; powerful, destructive storm; person higher in rank; very good
26. Cobbold Gorge	Spoonerisms	pack of lies, block of flats, blow your nose
27. Burial Styles (New Orleans)	The suffix *ism*	discrimination based on age; the practice of not going to work without a reason
28. Effects of Media Violence	*i.e.* or *e.g.*	No response required.
29. Natural Gemstones	*Other-world people*	Jovian, Uranian
30. Centrepoint	Comparative adjectives	better, best; worse, worst; more, most
31. How to play quoits	*made from or made of*	made of, made from
32. Cormorant	How to use *etc.*	No response required.
33. Coal and Coal Seam Gas	The suffix *cide*	king (monarch), a race (people), germs
34. One Touch could be Fatal	The asterisk	damn
35. Glenridge Bargain	Compound nouns	Examples: windscreen. black-market workhorse, carport, main road, panel van, tyre kickers, test drive
36. The Lighthouse	Compound verbs	double click, tap dance, waterproofs, dry freeze, drop kick
37. Avenue of Honour	Words from Mars	No response required.
38. Last Cab to Darwin	Compound adjectives	(1) Examples: true-life, outback, road-trip, right-to-die, weatherboard, slick-mouthed, medico-legal, born-and-bred
39. Discovery of Fairy Rings	*High or tall*	1. high, 2. tall, 3. tall, 4. high
40. Sir Edmund Hillary	Word oddities	When first letter is transferred to the end it becomes the reverse form of the word. (banana - ananab)

Understanding Year 8 Comprehension
A. Horsfield © Five Senses Education © W. Marlin

Notes